EUROPEAN UNION INTERNAL MARKET AND LABOUR LAW

Social Europe Series, Volume 19

EUROPEAN UNION INTERNAL MARKET AND LABOUR LAW: FRIENDS OR FOES?

Edited by
Marc De Vos

Contributors
Catherine Barnard
Philippe de Buck
Marc De Vos
Filip Dorssemont
Inge Govaere
John Monks
Armindo Silva
Dirk Sterckx

intersentia
Antwerp – Oxford – Portland

Distribution for the UK:
Hart Publishing Ltd.
16C Worcester Place
Oxford OX1 2JW
UK
Tel: +44 1865 51 75 30
Fax: +44 1865 51 07 10

Distribution for the USA and Canada:
International Specialized Book Services
920 NE 58th Ave Suite 300
Portland, OR 97213
USA
Tel: +1 800 944 6190 (toll free)
Tel: +1 503 287 3093
Fax: +1 503 280 8832
Email: info@isbs.com

Distribution for Switzerland and Germany:
Schulthess Verlag
Zwingliplatz 2
CH-8022 Zürich
Switzerland
Tel: +41 1 251 93 36
Fax: +41 1 261 63 94

Distribution for other countries:
Intersentia Publishers
Groenstraat 31
BE-2640 Mortsel
Belgium
Tel: +32 3 680 15 50
Fax: +32 3 658 71 21

European Union Internal Market and Labour Law: Friends or Foes?
Marc De Vos (ed.)

ISBN 978-90-5095-914-8
D/2009/7849/30
NUR 825

TABLE OF CONTENTS

THE RIGHT TO TAKE COLLECTIVE ACTION *V.* FUNDAMENTAL ECONOMIC FREEDOMS IN THE AFTERMATH OF *LAVAL* AND *VIKING*
Foes are forever!

PREFACE

The process of international economic integration commonly called 'globalisation' has an important labour market dimension. Labour or human capital as a production factor has been one of the key engines of globalisation ever since the fall of communism brought one and a half billion new workers into the global economy. The ability to tap into this phenomenal reservoir on an international scale, through a combination of investment, technology, transport, and migration, has confronted developed economies with new challenges and new forms of competition. Never before in human history was international labour market competition so global and so direct.

However, international economic integration has not coincided with international policy integration. As we have painfully observed during the financial crisis of 2008, economic globalisation has run ahead of regulatory globalisation, effectively generating a global market without a real global market framework. This is particularly true and perhaps inevitable for the labour market, thus both allowing and fuelling labour market competition between the participants in the global economy.

Within the context of the European Union the explosive mixture of economic integration and labour market competition has been further stirred by the enlargement of the EU towards the less economically developed former communist countries of Central and Eastern Europe. The enlargement of 2004, with additions in 2007, has opened the internal market of the European Union to a previously unknown diversity of labour standards. This historic process forms the general backdrop to the legal developments treated in this book.

This book explores the intricate, complex, and sometimes contentious relationship between the European Union's agenda for a free internal market and the protection of labour standards within the EU. The book cannot offer a definite or comprehensive analysis of an issue that is still largely developing. The immediate focus is on recent legal developments, both in case law and in legislation. But these developments are addressed in a more general approach that seeks to give an overall background and context. The result of a conference held in the aftermath of the instantly famous cases of *Laval* and *Viking*, the book also reports on a panel discussion between stakeholders.

May this book offer the reader some learning and inspiration on an issue that is both fundamental and symbolic for the future development of the European Union.

Marc De Vos
Ghent University
January 2009

CONTRIBUTORS

Catherine Barnard

Catherine Barnard MA (Cantab), LLM (EUI), PhD (Cantab) is Professor in European Union and Employment Law at the University of Cambridge and a fellow of Trinity College. She also holds a Jean Monnet chair of European Integration. Formerly she was the Jean Monnet Chair of European integration at the University of Southampton and Assistant Dean. She specialises in EC law, employment law and discrimination law. She is co-director of the Centre for European Legal Studies at Cambridge. She is author of *EC Employment Law* (Oxford, OUP, 2006, 3rd ed.), *The Substantive Law of the EU: The Four Freedoms*, (Oxford, OUP, 2007, 2nd ed.), editor of a collection of essays entitled *The Fundamentals of EU Law Revisited* (Oxford, 2007), editor of the *Cambridge Yearbook of European Legal Studies 2006–7* and *2007–8,* and co-editor of a collection of essays entitled *The Law of the Single European Market* Hart, 2002 (with Scott), of another volume entitled *The Future of Labour Law*, Hart, Oxford, 2004 (with Deakin and Morris) and of a book aimed at prospective law students entitled *What about Law?* (with Virgo and O'Sullivan).

Philippe de Buck

Philippe de Buck studied Law at the Catholic University of Louvain and Tax Law at ICHEC Brussels Management School. In 1987, after holding various functions within Agoria, a Belgian multisectoral federation for the technology industry, Philippe de Buck became CEO of Agoria. Since 2002 he has been Director General of BusinessEurope, the European employers' lobbying group.

Philippe de Buck is Member of the Board of Directors of ING Belgium and BASF Antwerp. He is also Chairman of the Fund of patronage of ING Belgium and Member of the Board of Directors of the Brussels Philharmonic Society.

Marc De Vos

Marc De Vos holds a Licentiate and Doctorate in Law (University of Ghent, 1993 and 2000), a Master in Social Law (Université Libre de Bruxelles, 1994), and a Master of Laws (Harvard University, 2000). He is a tenured professor of labour and employment law at the Ghent University Law School (www.law.ugent.be/social) and the University of Brussels (VUB – www.vub.ac.be/SORE/), where he teaches courses on Belgian, European and international employment and labour law. He serves as Director of the LLM programme in European Law at Ghent

University Law School (www.law.ugent.be/llm), and is also the director of the Itinera Institute, an independent and non-partisan institute for policy reform in Belgium, based in Brussels (www.itinerainstitute.org). His main areas of specialization include Belgian and European employment and labour law, labour market law and policy, and fundamental rights in both the constitutional and treaty context. About these and related legal and policy topics he frequently publishes, teaches, lectures and debates, both nationally and internationally, and both in academic, professional and policy circles, as well as in the media.

Filip Dorssemont

Filip Dorssemont holds a Licentiate and Doctorate in Law (Antwerp University). Furthermore, he has a bachelor in Philosophy (Antwerp University) and a Complementary Masters in Philosophy (Leuven University). He has been a Lecturer of Labour Law at Antwerp University and at Utrecht University. In 2008 he was able to return to Belgium due to the Ulysses Programme of the Fonds national de la recherche scientifique of the Communauté française (mandat d'impulsion Scientifique). In that capacity he is hosted by the Université Catholique de Louvain where he is a lecturer on labour law and industrial relations. He publishes about collective labour law, fundamental workers' rights and Community Labour Law.

Inge Govaere

Professor of European Law at Ghent University and Director of the European Legal Studies Department at the College of Europe, Bruges. Law studies at Ghent University (1987) and Ph.D at the European University Institute (E.U.I.) in Florence (Italy, 1994). Fulbright Scholar-in-Residence at Cornell University, N.Y. (USA, 1998). Visiting Professor, guest-lectures and conferences in Belgium and abroad, a.o. European University Institute (E.U.I., Firenze), Yale University (USA), Columbia University (N.Y., USA), Pittsburgh University (USA), Sao Paolo (Bresil), Lima (Perou), La Paz (Bolivia), Sofia (Bulgaria), Budapest (Hungary), Warsaw (Poland), Tunis (Tunesia), Ankara (Turkey). Publications include, inter alia, *The 1992 Challenge at National Level* (Nomos Verlagsgesellschaft, 1990), *The Use and Abuse of Intellectual Property Rights in EC Law* (Sweet & Maxwell, 1996), Entries in the second volume of *The Oxford Encyclopaedia of EC Law* (Oxford University Press, 2005), *European Legal Dynamics/Dynamiques Juridiques Européennes* (PIE, 2007), *Intellectual Property, Public Policy and International Trade* (PIE, 2007), *Intellectual Property, Market Power and the Public Interest* (PIE, 2008), *La Fonction Publique Communautaire* (Bruylant, 2008).

John Monks

John Monks is General Secretary of the European Trade Union Confederation. He has held that position since 2003. Previously, he was General Secretary of the

Trades Union Congress in Great Britain for 10 years. He has served on a range of public organisations in Britain and is a visiting Professor at the Manchester Business School. He writes periodically for the *Financial Times* and *the Guardian*.

Armindo Silva

Armindo Silva was born in Lisbon, on the 1st October 1950. He holds a degree in Economics by the Instituto Superior de Economia (University of Lisbon), an MA in Contemporary European Studies and a Ph.D in Economics by the University of Reading.

Before entering the Commission Armindo Silva was auxiliary professor at the Instituto Superior de Economia e Gestão (University of Lisbon) and taught European Studies at the Law faculty of the University of Coimbra. Armindo Silva is Acting Director for 'Social dialogue, social rights, working conditions and adaptation to change' since 1st January 2007. He is Head of the 'Labour law' Unit in the same Directorate. Armindo Silva started his career in the European Commission in 1988, at DG III (presently DG Enterprise), and in 1994 was appointed Head of Unit in DG Employment. He was responsible for employment policy, and for social protection and social inclusion policies, before taking over his present job. He took part in the launch of the Lisbon Strategy and the implementation of the Open Method of Coordination in the employment and social areas.

Dirk Sterckx

Dirk Sterckx studied German Filology at the University of Gent. After his studies he taught Dutch, English and German in various secondary schools in the Antwerp region. In 1975 he started his career as a journalist at the former public Belgian broadcasting company BRT where he became the EU correspondent in 1980.

On 13 June 1999 Dirk Sterckx was elected as a Member of the European Parliament and in 2004, he was re-elected. In the European Parliament, he follows the transport dossiers, environment dossiers and he is also the Chairman of the Delegation with China.

PART I
ANALYSIS

MODERNISATION OF THE INTERNAL MARKET: POTENTIAL CLASHES AND CROSSROADS WITH OTHER POLICIES

Prof. dr. Inge Govaere

Professor of European Law, Ghent University
Director European Legal Studies Department, College of Europe, Bruges

1. INTRODUCTION

The internal market is currently in the process of so-called 'modernisation'. It is also probably the most often invoked but perhaps least understood concept of European law. Its proponents may readily invoke the originally unifying and peacekeeping objective of the 'four freedoms' as well as the increasingly visible economic effects of the internal market process to support the steadily increasing expansion of its coverage.[1] Whereas a more critical view would tend to underline the potential interference of the expanding internal market with other pre-existing policies – often first formulated at national level – and question the ability of the former to take into account the specificities and needs of the latter. As is often the case, the truth may well lie somewhere in the middle. A balancing trick seems to be more opportune than a black or white approach, trying to reconcile different goals and get the best out of different policies.

The aim of this contribution is twofold. It is essentially to recall some of the main principles and orientations of the internal market concept specifically in its relation to other policies in general, thus not strictly limited to labour law. While at the same time making a preliminary assessment of the potential future impact of the current modernisation debate. It is structured around four main issues. Firstly, the dynamics of the internal market concept are briefly exposed, whereby in particular the question is raised what this current 'modernisation process' is all

---

1 For results, statistics and figures relating to the practical impact of the Internal Market, see Commission Staff Working Document "The Single Market: Review of Achievements", SEC (2007) 1521 of 20 November 2007. At p. 5 it is *inter alia* stated that "over the period 1992–2006, the estimated gains of the single market amount to 2.15% of the EU's GDP and 2.75 million extra jobs".

about and whether the Lisbon Reform Treaty may be expected to contribute in that respect. Secondly, it seems opportune to search for the boundaries or limits to internal market law, what could be called the 'no-go areas' or crossroads with other policies. A next step then is to establish what is covered by internal market law and what solutions may be found to reconcile at first sight conflicting policies. As a last resort and in case of persisting conflict, a last question purports to whether and to what extent other policy objectives nonetheless may be invoked to obtain a derogation from the internal market rules, and the potential influence of – or need for – harmonisation in that respect.

2. MODERNISING THE INTERNAL MARKET FOR THE 21ST CENTURY

At the event of the 21st century, several core areas of European law appear to be subject to a feverish quest for 'modernisation'. Only few may today still ignore the radical change in approach brought about by the call for modernisation[2] which led to the decentralization of European competition law in 2004.[3] Perhaps less known is that since 2007 also a modernisation process of internal market law appears to be firmly en route, calling for a quite fundamental change in approach also in this area. In its policy paper entitled "A vision for the Single Market of the 21st Century",[4] the European Commission openly pleads for a shift in focus away from the initial emphasis of removing barriers to cross-border trade in favour of a 'more impact-driven approach'. According to the Commission it is necessary to move away from the prior rather re-active vision of the internal market towards a more pro-active and policy-oriented approach, aimed to ensure "that markets function better, to the benefit of citizens and business".[5] This initial vision is further worked out in a series of initiatives bundled in the 'Single Market Review Package' which was rendered public on 20 November 2007.[6] In particular the Staff Working Document setting out the "Instruments for a modernized Single Market policy"[7] is enlightening with respect to the radical change in policy proposed by the Commission. It is pointed out that the current approach of "integration through the law", i.e. a combination of negative integration through direct

2 See the White Paper on Modernisation of the Rules Implementing Articles 81 and 82 of the EC Treaty *(formerly Articles 85 and 86 of the EC Treaty)*, O.J. C 132/1 of 12 May 1999.

3 Regulation (EC) No 1/2003 of 16 December 2002 on the Implementation of the Rules on Competition laid down in Articles 81 and 82 of the Treaty, O.J. L 1/1, 04 January 2003.

4 COM (2007) 60 final of 21 February 2007.

5 See also the Press Release, IP/07/2007 of 21/02/2007.

6 Communication from the Commission, "A Single Market for 21st Century Europe", COM (2007) 724 final of 20 November 2007.

7 SEC (2007) 1518 of 20 November 2007.

applicability of the four freedoms and a positive harmonisation-based integration, "can no longer be the Single Market's sole or primary ambition".[8] As for competition law, also for internal market law it is now held that the former more formalistic-legalistic approach should be set aside in favour of a more economic approach based on actively monitoring markets and using a mix of instruments in order to ensure that markets are made effectively open and competitive.[9]

The shift towards a more positive and interventionist approach to keep the markets open will of course in the future further accentuate the potential friction between internal market law and other policies. This is more or less so acknowledged by the Commission, through the recurrent emphasis throughout the Single Market Review Package that the Single Market goes "hand in hand with social and environmental policies to contribute to sustainable development goals" and needs to "encompass a strong social and environmental dimension".[10] A major challenge is thus to "find the right mix to allow trade to flourish while respecting labour law, health, safety and environmental standards".[11] It is not surprising, therefore, to find that on the same day and in the same Single Market Review Package a Commission Communication specifically deals with "Opportunities, access and solidarity: towards a new social vision for 21st century Europe".[12]

The Lisbon Reform Treaty, when it will enter into force, seems to provide the necessary legislative framework for such a more pro-active internal market policy which positively intertwines with other policies. On the one hand, among the objectives of the Union the new Article 3 TEU stipulates in paragraph 3 that: "The Union shall establish an internal market. It *shall work for* the sustainable development of Europe based on balanced economic growth and price stability, a highly competitive social market economy, aiming at full employment and social progress, and a high level of protection and the improvement of the quality of the environment. It *shall promote* scientific and technological advance."[13] This wording is very different from the current formulation used in Article 2 TEC. Since the Rome Treaty of 1957 the common market was always expressly considered to be instrumental in achieving such higher (*inter alia* social) objectives, but until now this was considered to be a 'natural' or 'passive'

8 Id., p. 5.

9 This new policy appears to be based to a large extent on the study by Ilzkotvitz, F., Dierx, A., Kovacs, V., and Sousa, N., "Steps towards a deeper economic integration: the Internal Market in the 21° Century: a contribution to the Single Market Review" *in* European Commission, *Economic Papers*, no. 271, January 2007.

10 See COM (2007) 724, *o.c.*, p. 4.

11 Id., p. 7.

12 COM (2007) 726 final of 20 November 2007.

13 Italics added.

consequence, rather than a 'positive' goal or target, of the establishment of the internal market.

On the other hand, the Lisbon Reform Treaty also introduces an important horizontal provision in Article 9 TFEU, stipulating that: "In defining and implementing its policies and activities, the Union shall take into account requirements linked to the promotion of a high level of employment, the guarantee of adequate social protection, the fight against social exclusion, and a high level of education, training and protection of human health". This obligation appears to be much larger in extent and coverage than the current reference to be found in Article 95(3) TEC, relating to the need for the Commission to take into account a high level of protection relating to health, safety, environmental protection and consumer protection when proposing harmonisation measures related to the internal market. It is still not totally clear, however, how a more economic and efficiency based internal market vision as expressed by the Commission, will in the long run better go hand in hand with the promotion of non-economic policies, such as in the social and environmental field.

Both the new policy of the Commission and the forthcoming Treaty amendments may thus be expected in the future to lead to a bigger convergence and overlap between internal market policy and other policies (in particular in the social and environmental sphere) than is currently the case. The big challenge will of course be to ensure that the various policies coincide and are mutually supportive in the long run. This is certainly not to be taken for granted. Already now, under the current internal market approach which, as pointed out by the Commission, is essentially reactive and legalistic and mainly aims at eliminating obstacles to the four freedoms between the Member States, the choice between clash or crossroad is sometimes walking a tightrope.

3. IN SEARCH OF THE LIMITS TO THE INTERNAL MARKET

Before looking at the current coexistence and potential interference of internal market and other policies, it is opportune to recall that the concept of the internal market is not a bottomless pit nor a mere policy instrument. It is a concept of Community law which, as such, is subject to judicial review by the European Court of Justice. Article 14 TEC broadly defines the internal market as "an area without internal frontiers in which the free movement of goods, persons, services and capital is ensured in accordance with the provisions of this Treaty". The importance of having this definition, even if it is one of the very few definitions expressly provided by the EC Treaty, should not be overestimated. It cannot be ignored that the ECJ has held in the *Wijsenbeek* case,[14] in relation to the free movement of persons prior to the Amsterdam Treaty, that the possibility to also effectively invoke the fundamental freedoms in order to oppose the application of national law is neither automatic nor unconditional. It first of all necessitates the existence of more detailed Treaty provisions, agreed upon by all the Member States and ratified according to their own constitutional rules, which may then constitute the proper legal basis for action. With the Amsterdam Treaty and subject to opt-outs for certain Member States in relation to the external frontiers for persons,[15] the more detailed Treaty provisions have now been put into place with respect to all four originally mentioned fundamental freedoms, so that this first hurdle no longer seems to be too difficult to take.[16] It is worth mentioning, however, that the Commission currently pleads for the promotion of the free movement of knowledge and innovation as a 'fifth freedom'.[17] Yet there is currently no mention of such a fifth fundamental freedom in the internal market definition of the EC Treaty (nor is it taken up, as such, in the Lisbon Reform Treaty), let alone that more detailed provisions have been agreed upon which could form the direct legal basis for internal market action in that field.[18]

Equally important is the understanding that policy is not necessarily tantamount to law and can anyhow not successfully dispense with the latter. This is probably the most interesting lesson to be drawn from the *Tobacco Advertising Directive* judgment of the ECJ.[19] The ECJ recalled the importance of the principle of attributed competence, laid down in Article 5 TEC (and maintained in the Lisbon Reform Treaty), as a guiding principle for the lawfulness of all EC action. It clarified that it does not suffice that there is a qualified majority, or for that matter even political consensus, among Member States to proceed through Community channels. The Community in general, and the internal market in particular, is not just a toy in the hands of the Member States to be used at will. Contrary to what is often believed, the ECJ underlined that the EC has no general regulatory competence, even in a field which is so important to the EC as the internal market.

14 Case C-378/97, *Wijsenbeek, ECR* (1999) I-6207.

15 See Hanf, D., Munoz, R., (eds.), *La Libre Circulation des Personnes : Etats des Lieux et Perspectives*, PIE Peter Lang, 2007, and in particular in relation to the opt-out countries the contribution in that book by Munoz, R., "Les cas particuliers des ressortissants communautaires des pays "out" (Royaume-Uni, Irlande et Danemark)", at pp. 75–97.

16 For an analysis of the evolution of the internal market concept and its underlying principles, see Barnard, C., *The substantive law of the EU: The Four Freedoms*, Oxford University Press, 2004.

17 See COM (2007) 724, *o.c.*, p. 9.

18 To the contrary, Article 30 EC Treaty still lists industrial and commercial property among the exceptions to the free movement of goods.

19 Case C-376/98, *Germany v. European Parliament and Council, ECR* (2000) I-8419.

The EC only has the competence to take regulatory measures *to the extent necessary* to improve the conditions and functioning of the internal market or to prevent the emergence of future obstacles to trade.[20] Whereas at the time of the judgment the reactive vision of the internal market as removing barriers to trade clearly prevailed, a similar reasoning could still apply to a more proactive vision of the internal market, more actively leading to opening up markets. Such a 'necessity' test essentially delimits the scope of internal market measures in function of a case-by-case elimination – or prevention – of obstacles to intra-Community trade.

At the same time, the ECJ also clarified that this case-by-case test is not only necessary but also sufficient. As soon as it is shown that EC action is needed to eliminate barriers to intra-Community trade, to open up markets, or to prevent the emergence of obstacles to trade,[21] then the necessary harmonisation measures may be taken on the basis of Article 95 TEC. The fact that this incidentally interferes with other 'higher' objectives or policies, such as the protection of public health which is expressly listed in the EC Treaty as a complementary competence excluding EC harmonisation,[22] cannot successfully be invoked to oppose targeted internal market harmonisation. Internal market harmonisation measures may thus take into account other – especially horizontal – policies such as public health but may not be taken specifically for the sake of protecting the latter objectives. This solution given by the Court appears to be well-balanced and is to be warmly welcomed. It does not allow the internal market to unduly impinge on other policies, whereas it prevents other policies from paralyzing all internal market progress. The ECJ has thus opted for a crossroad approach between the internal market and other important policies rather than acknowledge the alleged existence of a clash provoked by – at first sight – conflicting Treaty provisions.

The *Tobacco Advertising Directive* case unequivocally shows that the EC, in the current state of the Treaties, has no general regulatory competence with respect to the internal market. It is not surprising, therefore, that the internal market provisions may also not be interpreted as conferring a general regulatory competence to deal with other policies, regardless of whether or not the Treaty expressly reserves competence for the Member States in those fields. An encroachment of the internal market rules on other policies will only be permitted

---

20 *Id.*, see in particular at para 83–86.

21 The possibility to use Article 95 TEC to prevent also the emergence of obstacles to trade has been criticized, inter alia subsequent to the second Tobacco Advertising Directive case, see Ludwigs, M., annotation to Case C-380/93, *Germany v. European Parliament and Council* (Tobacco Advertising II; ECR (2006) I-11573), *C.M.L.Rev.* (2007) 1159.

22 Article 152 TEC; Germany heavily relied on this Treaty provision to argue the annulment of the Tobacco Advertising Directive.

by the ECJ 'to the extent necessary' to safeguard the four fundamental freedoms. A recent example is to be found in the *Eind* case.[23] Here the question was raised to what extent the internal market rules could curtail the application of national migration laws with respect to family members of own nationals. It concerned a Dutch national who was joined by his daughter directly from Surinam while working in the UK, and the status of his daughter and this family reunification upon his return to the Netherlands. The ECJ held that "the right of the migrant worker to return and reside in the Member State of which he is a national, after being gainfully employed in another Member State, is conferred by EC law, *to the extent necessary* to ensure the *useful effect* of the right to free movement of workers under Article 39 EC and the provision adopted to give effect to that right, such as those laid down in Regulation No. 1612/68".[24] Internal market rules thus interfere only to strike down the sharp edges of national migration laws, *in casu* those which pose barriers to family reunification and thus are liable to undermine the free movement of persons in conflict with EC law.[25] The criterion of 'to the extent necessary to safeguard internal market objectives' thus determines the place and the importance of the crossroad with other policies. The crucial question thus becomes to determine when the ECJ considers that it is indeed 'necessary' to apply internal market rules to curtail other policies.

4. THE 'NECESSITY' TO APPLY INTERNAL MARKET RULES

Other than simply referring back to the definition given in Article 14 TEC, it is not all that easy to clearly state what is precisely covered by the concept of the internal market. Putting aside the Commission's current plea for the acknowledgement of a fifth freedom (see above), one may even contest that the internal market today relates to 'four' clearly distinct freedoms, as Article 14 TEC would seem to indicate.[26] Also the gradual expansion of the scope of Community competence to include non-economic matters puts a lot of strain on the original internal market concept. For instance, the question may be raised whether the free movement of persons, which was originally inserted in the 1957 Rome Treaty in relation to workers and self-employed persons, today also includes the free movement of EU citizens at large. Support for such a statement may be found in

---

23 Case C-291/05, *Ministerie voor Vreemdelingenzaken en Integratie v. R.M.G. Eind*, Judgment of 11 December 2007, nyp.

24 *Id*, at para 32, italics added.

25 *Id*, para 37.

26 See also Hatzopoulos, V., "Trente ans après les arrêts fondamentaux de 1974, les quatre libertés : quatre ?", *in* Demaret, P., Govaere, I., Hanf, D., *European Legal Dynamics*, P.I.E. Peter Lang, 2007, p. 185.

the adoption of secondary law, and in particular Directive 2004/38, which takes into consideration criteria such as nationality and duration of stay and not just the performance of an economic activity.[27] The latter appears to be in keeping with the important development in the case law of the ECJ relating to citizenship of the Union and the rights to movement attached thereto, initiated with the insertion of Article 18 TEC in the Maastricht Treaty.[28]

However, recent case law of the ECJ in relation to internal market law *strictu sensu* still seems to emphasise the importance of the economic rationale of the internal market, whereby it is above all the free movement of economic commodities that needs to be safeguarded and a level playing field in terms of competition created. An illustration is to be found in the *Meca Medina* case of July 2006 concerning doping control rules for swimmers adopted *inter alia* by the International Olympic Committee.[29] Whereas the ECJ held differently for the application of the competition rules,[30] with respect to the internal market rules it firmly reiterated that the decisive element to bring sporting activities within the ambit of free movement of persons and services is the existence of an economic activity in the sense of Article 2 TEC.[31] According to established case law, the scope of the rules on workers and services definitely covers cases "where the sporting activity takes the form of gainful employment or the provision of services for remuneration",[32] such as is the case for professional or semi-professional sportsmen. The ECJ now clarifies that this does not automatically entail that also all sporting rules relating to such sportsmen are covered by the internal market rules. Rules which concern 'purely sporting interests', this is in particular "rules or practices justified on non-

---

27 Directive 2004/38/EC of the European Parliament and of the Council of 29 April 2004 on the Right of Citizens of the Union and their Family Members to Move and Reside Freely within the Territory of the Member States amending Regulation (EEC) No. 1612/68 and repealing Directives 64/221/EEC, 68/360/EEC, 72/194/EEC, 73/148/EEC, 75/34/EEC, 75/35/EEC, 90/364/EEC, 90/365/EEC and 93/96/EEC (Text with EEA relevance), O.J. L 158/77 of 30 April 2004. Economic activity remains an important criterion with respect to the conditions attached to the free movement, in particular in the period between 3 months and 5 years.

28 See Hanf, D., "Le développement de la citoyenneté de l'Union Européenne", *in* Hanf, D., Munoz, R., (eds.), *La Libre Circulation des Personnes : Etats des Lieux et Perspectives*, PIE Peter Lang, 2007, pp. 15–27; Mather, J., "The Court of Justice and the Union Citizen", *European Law Journal* (2005) 722–743; Carrera, S., "What does free movement mean in theory and practice in an enlarged EU?", *European Law Journal* (2005) 699–721.

29 Case C-519/04 P, *Meca Medina*, 18 July 2006, *ECR* (2006) I-6991.

30 Case C-519/04 P, *o.c.*, esp. at para 32–33, where the ECJ states that the CFI has made an error of law by also automatically excluding purely sporting rules from the scope of Articles 81–82 TEC. On this issue, see A. Vermeersch, "All's Fair in Sport and Competition? The Application of EC Competition Rules to Sport", *JCER* (2007) 238–254.

31 Case C-519/04 P, *o.c.*, para 22.

32 Case C-519/04 P, *o.c.*, para 23.

economic grounds which relate to the particular nature and context of certain sporting events" will not be precluded by the internal market rules.[33]

An important lesson to be drawn from the *Meca Medina* case is that, today, it is still important to determine on a case-by-case basis whether or not a contested rule effectively relates to an 'economic activity' or embodies 'economic aspects', as a pre-condition for the internal market rules to apply. This means that also many non-economic aspects of policies other than sports, or rules which 'purely' relate to, for instance, social, environmental, or public health policies, will not at all be affected by the four freedoms. The interface or crossroad between internal market and other policies is thus for the time being limited to economic aspects of the latter and does not provoke a fully overlapping (and thus a high potential for clash) situation. As the sporting cases illustrate, it is not always easy, however, to apply this criterion in practice and to determine what exactly is a 'purely sporting' matter that will continue to fall outside the scope of the internal market rules. It may not be settled through a 'black-and-white' approach which can be determined in abstracto, but necessarily warrants a tailor-made approach taking into account the context of each specific case. The fact that in many cases internal market concerns are thus expressed, may easily create the wrong impression that the internal market is always and systematically also involved and is by virtue of some kind of creeping competence *de facto* taking over other policies.

An additional question is whether it is also 'sufficient' that it is established in any given case that there is an economic activity in the sense of Article 2 TEC for the internal market rules to apply and potentially 'take over' other policies. The fact that the ECJ has for a long time, subsequent to the *Cassis de Dijon* case,[34] seemed to favour this view probably explains the fears of an undue encroachment of internal market law on other policies. This line of case law has also contributed to the impression that other 'higher' policies could only be maintained when justified by way of a derogation to the internal market rules. It is no secret that the ECJ has for quite some time struggled with the necessity to find workable criteria to delimit the scope of the internal market rules.[35]

As mentioned before, the internal market rules are essentially aimed at removing obstacles to intra-Community trade and not at a deregulation, as such, at a national level. The fact that discriminatory measures are such obstacles to be

33 Case C-519/04 P, *o.c.*, para 25–26.

34 Case 120/78, *Rewe-Zentrale (Cassis de Dijon)*, *ECR* (1979) 649.

35 For a critical view, see a.o. White, E., "In search of the limits to Article 30 of the EEC Treaty" *C.M.L.Rev.* (1989) 235; Mortelmans, K., "Article 30 of the EEC Treaty and legislation relating to market circumstances: time to consider a new definition", *C.M.L.Rev.* (1991) 115.

targeted by the internal market rules goes largely uncontested. Openly or indirectly discriminatory measures are in principle always in breach of the internal market rules. Yet this is less evident for the inclusion of indistinctly applicable rules in the scope of the four freedoms. Non-discriminatory measures may, nonetheless, also affect the intra-Community movement of economic commodities, simply because the legislation may be different from Member State to Member State. Acknowledging this either leads to all economic regulation to be more or less automatically covered by the internal market rules, which was the situation subsequent to the *Cassis De Dijon* ruling of the ECJ.[36] Or else workable criteria need to be found to distinguish between, on the one hand, those indistinctly applicable measures that effectively affect the four freedoms and should be covered by the internal market rules and, on the other hand, those that have no such effect and thus should remain outside the scope of the internal market rules. The latter is the more difficult exercise that was firmly initiated by the ECJ in the well-known *Keck and Mithouard* case[37] and which has inspired much debate.[38] Initially the ECJ seemed to opt for a more formalistic criterion, distinguishing between different types of indistinctly applicable measures, such as product requirements and selling modalities, to trigger or not the application of internal market rules.[39] This has more or less quickly evolved towards the adoption of a more functional, more workable, and better accepted criterion of 'market access'.[40] Today it can be said that only those indistinctly applicable rules that render the access to the labour, product, capital or services market of another Member State more difficult are covered by the internal market rules and principles. The other indistinctly applicable measures do not come within the ambit of the four freedoms, even if they relate to an economic activity.

The adoption of the more functional criterion of restriction of market access by the ECJ illustrates that the situation in the market and the necessity to remove existing obstacles to the free movement, or to keep the internal market open, is currently already more important than the legal qualification of a contested measure. From that perspective, it is not totally clear what the difference is, in practical terms, with the 'impact-based' approach which is newly proposed by the Commission in the Single Market Review.[41] Perhaps the fact that it is still national

---

36 Case 120/78, *Rewe-Zentrale (Cassis de Dijon), ECR* (1979) 649.

37 Joined Cases C-267 & 268/91, *Keck and Mithouard, ECR* (1993) I-6097.

38 See, for instance, Weatherill, S., "After Keck: Some thoughts on how to clarify the clarification" *C.M.L.Rev.* (1996) 885; Maduro, M., "Harmony and dissonance in free movement", in *Cambridge Yearbook of European Legal Studies* (2001) 315.

39 Joined Cases C-267 & 268/91, *o.c.*, at para 15–16.

40 See for instance the *Alpine Investment* judgment, which relates to services but where the ECJ seems to give a functional reading of its formalistic Keck approach in relation to free movement of goods, Case C-384/93, *Alpine Investment, ECR* (1995) I-1141.

41 See COM (2007) 724, *o.c.*

legislation that is scrutinized upon market access restrictions *'ex post'*, rather than that the practical situation in the market, as such, is evaluated *'ex ante'* to the occurrence of a real problem for the market? The Commission calls for a better monitoring and a more pro-active policy, through *inter alia* the screening of targeted sectors and putting into place a consumer scoreboard.[42] It should not be forgotten, however, that not only the Commission itself[43] but also – if not foremost – individuals and undertakings already act as primary enforcers of internal market law through the direct applicability and effective invocation before the national courts of the internal market rules.

There are currently at least three different ways to tackle problems of potential obstacles to intra-Community trade, depending on whether one is faced with an *ex post* or *ex ante* situation and on whether one seeks to bring the problem in, rather than keep it outside, internal market law. In the absence of EC harmonisation, many *'ex post'* situations relating to indistinctly applicable measures may efficiently be tackled through the application of the principle of mutual recognition by the national courts.[44] In that way the application of double or multiple standards can easily be avoided. This solution is of course not possible for discriminatory measures or when higher objectives mentioned in the Treaty or mandatory requirements, including those relating to other policies such as relating to social, environmental or public health, are successfully invoked (see *infra*, pt. 5). In that case the most straightforward solution appears to be to create (more or less) uniform conditions throughout the internal market through the negotiation and adoption of positive harmonisation measures at EU level, based on Article 95 TEC. As mentioned before,[45] the ECJ has held that such measures should be specifically targeted to eliminate identified – or to prevent the occurrence of identifiable – barriers to trade. With the so-called 'New Approach', combining

---

42 COM (2007) 724 final, *o.c.*, at p. 11–12. See also the Commission Staff Working Document on "Implementing the new methodology for product market and sector monitoring: Results of a first sector screening", SEC (2007) 1517 of 21 November 2007, where it is held at p. 5 that "This in-depth market monitoring could be used a a strategic tool to help define the priority measures for a better functioning Single Market".

43 See also the Commission Communication on "A Europe of Results – applying Community law", COM 52007) 502 final, which sets out the new policy of the Commission on the application of EC law. Here a more decentralized control and enforcement system is proposed with a 'monitoring' and 'referral' system of complaints by the Commission and the possibility to engage in priority-setting. For a critical view on this Communication, see Munoz, R., "La 'nouvelle approche' de la Commission concernant l'application du droit communautaire : Grandeurs et décadence des mécanismes de contrôle", *Europe* (2007) 4.

44 On the obligation of the Member States to write the principle of mutual recognition in their national laws, see Case C-184/96, *Commission v. France (Foie Gras), ECR* (1998) I-6197 and Case C-24/00, *Commission v. France (Vitamins), ECR* (2004) I-1277.

45 See *supra* the *Tobacco Advertising Directive* case.

positive and negative harmonisation,[46] this exercise is in practice further limited to those situations where the principle of mutual recognition (which is expressly written in the harmonisation measure) does not already remedy the market access restrictions.[47]

Another and in some circumstances probably better solution is of course to increase the awareness about potential implications of the internal market with policy makers in other fields. If, for instance, social, environmental and public health policy instruments are drafted with due regard to the internal market principles of non-discrimination and market access, then there will be little or no need for an 'ex post' interference of internal market law at all. It is significant that the Commission in its Communication on "Opportunities, access and solidarity: towards a new social vision for 21st Century Europe" *inter alia* draws attention to issues of market access and non-discrimination in the social field.[48] It is perhaps to be regretted that this 'external' approach is not truly developed also in the Staff Working Document on the "Instruments for a modernized single market policy", in spite of a rather promising heading "Developing stronger synergies with other EU and national policies".[49] Instead, much attention is paid to promote a mix of tools and in particular the use of more flexible – read 'non-binding and soft law' – instruments. It is, however, doubtful that a "more consistent and coherent approach to the use of non-binding tools" is indeed sufficient to dispel the stated European Parliaments objections to the use of such tools "on grounds of institutional balance and democracy".[50] It is one thing to plead for a more impact-based internal market, it is something totally different to move away from an internal market based on the rule of law.[51]

46 On the regulatory aspects of the internal market, see Joerges, C., "Free Trade with hazardous products? The emergence of transnational governance with eroding state government", *European Foreign Affairs Review* (2005) 553. At p. 554 he presents the argument "that the completion of the Internal Market required institutional innovations which established symbiotic relationships between markets and regulatory policies which now represent a cornerstone of European multilevel governance".

47 I have maintained elsewhere that one of the problems of the services directive is precisely that it does not provide the necessary harmonisation of obstacles to market access but instead codifies exceptions to the free movement. This is most likely due to the fact that as a starting presumption, it was considered that it was the principle of mutual recognition that needed to be reformulated in a country of origin principle combined with the horizontal scope of the measure, see Govaere, I., "De Bolkestein richtlijn in de context van het acquis communautaire: evolutie of revolutie?", *Tijdschrift voor Sociaal Recht* (2006) 3. Another issue is of course the possibility for Member States to derogate from harmonisation measures subsequent to Article 95(4) and (5) TEC.

48 COM (2007) 726 final of 20 November 2007.

49 SEC 52007° 1518 of 20 November 2007, pt. 3.4.

50 *Id.*, at p. 10 ff.

51 This development of using non-binding instruments to formulate policies, sometimes without proper legal basis, is not limited to the internal market. See for instance concerning human

5. 'HIGHER' POLICY OBJECTIVES AS DEROGATIONS FROM INTERNAL MARKET RULES

In the Community system of checks and balances, it is not because a measure comes within the ambit of the internal market rules that it is also automatically prohibited. A measure relating to an economic activity in the sense of Article 2 TEC and containing discriminatory or market access restrictive elements may under certain conditions benefit from a derogation to the four freedoms in order to protect higher objectives. Whereas the EC Treaty already expressly mentions certain exceptions, such as relating to public policy, public security or public health in Article 30, 39 and 46 TEC, the possibility to invoke other higher objectives, the so-called mandatory requirements, was already early on acknowledged by the ECJ in the *Cassis de Dijon* case.[52] More recently one may discern two new and potentially important developments in the case law. Firstly, the ECJ has in some cases opened the door to derogations based on the protection of fundamental rights. Secondly, the ECJ acknowledges that the insertion of new and distinct policies in the Treaties call for a renewed search for balance.

These new developments do not alter the importance of first trying to keep a measure outside the scope of internal market law. The application for a derogation to internal market rules brings the measure within the scope of judicial review by the ECJ, regardless of whether or not it concerns a Member States competence. By virtue of the crossroads established with internal market law, the ECJ will thus acquire a right to review Member States legislation in other fields. However, it may not substitute its view for that of the Member States but only determine whether the measure is justified in view of the higher objective invoked and proportional.[53] The latter essentially means that there is no alternative measure less restrictive of intra-Community trade. Member States may in principle invoke all higher objectives, including for instance the protection of workers or public health, as long as they are non-economic in nature. Even derogations to harmonisation measures are possible but strictly under the conditions of Articles

rights: Govaere, I. and Van Bossuyt, A., "Le commerce à visage de plus en plus humain ? Les droits de l'homme dans la politique commerciale commune", *in* Candela Soriano M. (ed), *Les droits de l'homme dans les politiques de l'Union européenne*, Brussel, De Boeck/Larcier, 2006, pp. 225–254; concerning intellectual property rights: Govaere, I., "With eyes wide shut: the EC strategy to enforce intellectual property rights abroad", *in* Dashwood/Maresceau (eds.) *Law and Practice of EC external relations*, Cambridge University Press, 2008, (at press).

52 Case 120/78, *o.c.*

53 In principle mandatory requirements additionally have to be indistinctly applicable although the ECJ does not seem to be consistently strict on the respect of that criterion.

95(4) and (5) TEC. In practice, however, derogations to internal market rules are of course most often invoked with respect to non-harmonised measures.

The starting position to take the crossroad between internal market rules and other policies is fundamentally different when establishing the scope of application of the four freedoms or when granting the derogations thereto. As mentioned before, internal market rules will only curtail other policies 'to the extent necessary' to eliminate obstacles to the four freedoms. Yet as it concerns a basic rule, the concept of 'obstacles to intra-Community trade' will receive a wide interpretation (economic activity plus discrimination or market access restriction). Similarly, once it is established that the contested measure comes within the scope of the internal market rules, then derogations will only be permitted 'to the extent necessary' to achieve the higher objective invoked. But as it concerns an exception to a fundamental rule, the latter will necessarily receive a much more restrictive interpretation. This does not mean that the balance will always and automatically turn out in favour of the internal market rules to the detriment of higher objectives. The acceptance by the ECJ of the precautionary principle with respect to the public health protection is a good illustration in that respect.[54] Conversely, the balance will also not always and automatically turn out in favour of the higher objective invoked.[55]

In a recent line of cases, among which are *Schmidberger,*[56] *Omega,*[57] *Viking*[58] and *Laval*[59], the ECJ has pointed to the possibility for Member States to invoke the protection of fundamental rights, such as the right to demonstrate or the right to strike, as a derogation to the internal market rules. At first sight this development seems to be welcome as it recognises that fundamental rights may be higher objectives to the four freedoms. The drawback is, however, that in so doing fundamental rights are also put in the balance with the four fundamental freedoms. An additional problem is that the ECJ may be called upon to review human rights standards in national measures which do not strictly speaking fall within the ambit of Community law.

The second recent development seems to be less problematic. Whereas for determining the scope of the internal market it is still mainly an economic

54 On the origin and importance of this principle, see Vos, E., "Le principe de précaution et le droit alimentaire de l'Union européenne", *RIDE* (2002) 219.

55 See for instance the so-called Strawberries case, where the ECJ rejected the public security exception invoked by France, Case C-265/95, *Commission v. France, ECR* (1997) I-6959.

56 Case C-112/00, *Schmidberger, ECR* (2003) I-5659.

57 Case C-36/02, *Omega, ECR* (2004) I-9609.

58 Case C-438/05, *Viking*, Judgment of 11 December 2007, nyp.

59 Case C-341/05, *Laval*, Judgment of 18 December 2007, nyp.

rationale that prevails, for the derogations the ECJ increasingly takes into account the dynamics of European integration, subsequent to Treaty amendments, and in particular the fact that the EC has now also acquired competence in non-economic matters. For instance, in the recent *Viking* case, the ECJ attached a great importance to the current formulation used in Articles 2 and 3 TEC, which puts the social policy on the same footing as internal market policy.[60] Some may regret that the ECJ does not infer from this evolution that social policy is now totally to be kept outside the reach of internal market law. The step taken by the ECJ is nonetheless not negligible. It unequivocally stated that "(s)ince the Community has thus not only an economic but also social purpose, the rights under the provisions of the Treaty on the free movement of goods, persons, services and capital must be balanced against the objectives pursued by social policy".[61] The new and more pro-active formulation of the internal market objective in the Lisbon Reform Treaty as mentioned before (*supra* pt. 2) can only further fuel this kind of considerations favourable to other non-economic policies.

6. CONCLUSION

In the Single Market Review, the Commission pleads for the promotion of synergies between the internal market and other policies. This is to be warmly welcomed, although the two-way street could be more emphasised. It cannot be ignored that the internal market has and will continue at times to interfere with other policies. Conversely other policies may sometimes be successfully invoked to derogate from internal market rules. This is not tantamount to accepting that different policies should merge into one big and all overriding policy or that one policy should take the upper hand. The big challenge is to provide the necessary crossroads, to search for complementarities and to establish criteria for reaching an acceptable balance on a case-by-case basis. Purists from either side may regret such an interaction and plainly refute this discussion. Yet a plea for a strict separation between the different policies does not appear to be very realistic, nor very constructive, in the current state of Community law. With the modernisation package and the Lisbon Reform Treaty a more pro-active internal market approach in closer association with other policies seems to be well on its way for the years to come.

---

60 Case C-438/05, *o.c.*, para 78.
61 Case C-438/05, *o.c.*, para 79.

INTERNAL MARKET *V.* LABOUR MARKET: A BRIEF HISTORY

Catherine BARNARD

Trinity College, Cambridge, Professor in EU Law and Employment Law
Jean Monnet Chair of European Union Law

1. INTRODUCTION

Viking[1] and *Laval*[2] have brought the question of the balance between the EC internal market rules and national labour law rules into sharp focus. In this chapter I will argue that, in the original version of the Treaty, the rules on the common market were seen as wholly distinct from those concerning social policy. Indeed, there was very little social policy actually in the EEC Treaty because social policy was seen as a national matter going to the heart of sovereignty and national identity. This will be discussed in section 2. However, as companies began to take advantage of their rights of free movement the two worlds inevitably began to collide (section 3). Inevitably, the task has fallen to the Court to address this problem, although the legislator has also been forced to attend to these issues, particularly in the context of the Services Directive. Section 4 therefore looks at the various tools which have been used to address the conflict between national employment law and EC free movement rights. Section 5 concludes with an examination of how those tools have been used in *Viking* and *Laval*.

2. THE TREATY OF ROME: TWO SEPARATE WORLDS

2.1. FREE MOVEMENT

The original EEC Treaty had as its task the establishment of a common market and the progressive approximation of the economic policies of the Member

1 Case C-438/05 *Viking Line ABP* v. *The International Transport Workers' Federation, the Finnish Seaman's Union* [2005] EWHC 1222 (QBD) and [2005] EWCA Civ. 1299 (Court of Appeal) [2007] ECR I-10779.

2 Case C-341/05 *Laval un Partneri Ltd* v. *Svenska Byggnadsarbetareförbundet* [2007] ECR I-11767.

States.[3] Thus, the Treaty provisions on the four freedoms (now) Articles 28, 39, 43, 49 and 56 were intended to open up national markets to competition from elsewhere in the EU, allowing resources to move to the area where they could be most efficiently used. Therefore industries needing a lot of labour were able to locate to areas where labour was plentiful, those industries relying on heavy materials to locate near places where those materials were produced or delivered and those industries requiring heavy investment to states where capital was freely available and financial charges were lowest.[4] This virtuous circle was to lead to salary levels and interest rates being equalised when the demand for labour or the demand for capital increased.[5] So, the thinking underpinning the EEC Treaty was that improved working conditions would be the consequence of market integration, not a prerequisite to it, an idea caught in the original Article 117 EEC: an improvement in working conditions would '*ensue* not only from the functioning of the Common Market… but also… from the approximation of provisions laid down by law, regulation or administrative action'.[6] Viewed from this perspective, there was little need for the EEC to have a social dimension: social policy was left to the Member States.

The Spaak report was also opposed to general intervention in the social sphere, although it did acknowledge that action should be taken to correct or eliminate the effect of specific distortions which advantage or disadvantage certain branches of activity. By way of example, the authors cited a list of areas for possible intervention, including working conditions of labour such as the relationship between the salaries of men and women, working time, overtime and paid holidays, and different policies relating to credit. The French government strongly endorsed the view that there was a need for federal intervention in these areas. With its strong legislation on equal pay for men and women and its more generous rules on paid holidays, France was concerned that the additional costs borne by French industry would make French goods uncompetitive in the Common Market.[7]

These different perspectives were reflected in the ragbag of provisions contained in the (inaptly named) Title on Social Policy.[8] Articles 117 and 118 EEC (new and amended Articles 137 and 140) on the need to improve working

---

3 Article 2 EEC.

4 Rapport des Chefs de Délégations, Comité Intergouvernemental, 21 April 1956.

5 *Ibid.*

6 Emphasis added.

7 These arguments are considered more fully in Barnard, *EC Employment Law* (OUP, Oxford, 2006), 3rd ed., ch. 1.

8 Although included in a title entitled 'social policy', it is in fact misleading to use this terminology. The 'social policy' Title made no provision for what is generally agreed to be the central core of social policy: social insurance, public assistance, health and welfare services, education and housing policy. There was also no evidence of the creation of a European welfare state to replace the national welfare states, and certainly no evidence of cradle-to-grave protection.

conditions and co-operation between states, even if textually broad, were legally shallow, reflecting the Spaak preference for laissez-faire,[9] while Article 119 (new Article 141) on equal pay and Article 120 (new Article 142) on paid holiday schemes and the third protocol on 'Certain Provisions Relating to France' on working hours and overtime,[10] were specific provisions designed to protect French industry.[11]

The essentially protectionist function of these provisions was recognised by Advocate General Dutheillet de Lamothe in *Defrenne (No. 1)*.[12] He said that although Article 141 had a social objective it also had an economic objective,

> for in creating an obstacle to any attempt at 'social dumping' by means of the use of female labour less well paid than male labour, it helped to achieve one of the fundamental objectives of the common market, the establishment of a system ensuring that 'competition is not distorted'.

He continued that 'This explains why Article [141] of the Treaty is of a different character from the articles which precede it in the chapter of the Treaty devoted to social provisions'.

The Court echoed these sentiments in its landmark judgment in *Defrenne (No 2)*:[13]

> Article [141] pursues a double aim. *First*, ... the aim of Article [141] is to avoid a situation in which undertakings established in states which have actually implemented

9 Forman, 'The Equal Pay Principle under Community Law' (1982) 1 *LIEI* 17.

10 This provided that the Commission was to authorize France to take protective measures where the establishment of the Common Market did not result, by the end of the first stage, in the basic number of hours beyond which overtime was paid and the average rate of additional payment for overtime industry corresponding to the average obtaining in France in 1956. It does not seem that France has called upon this safeguard clause: Budiner, *Le Droit de la femme l'Égalité de salaire et la Convention No. 100 de l'organisation internationale du travail* (Librairie Générale de Droit et de Jurisprudence, Paris, 1975).

11 According to the French Advocate General Dutheillet de Lamothe in Case 80/70 *Defrenne (No. 1)* v. *SABENA* [1971] ECR 445, 'It appears to be France which took the initiative, but the article [119] necessitated quite long negotiations'. However, the content of Article 119 was strongly influenced by ILO Convention No. 100 on equal pay. See Hoskyns, *Integrating Gender* (Verso, London, 1996) and Arnull, *The European Union an dits Court of Justice* (OUP, Oxford, 2006), 534–540.

12 Case 80/70 [1971] ECR 445. In Case 69/80 *Worringham and Humphreys* v. *Lloyd's Bank* [1981] ECR 767 Advocate General Warner again referred back to Advocate General Dutheillet de Lamothe's statement in *Defrenne (No. 1)* that the first purpose of Article 119 was to 'avoid a situation in which undertakings established in Member States with advanced legislation on the equal treatment of men and women suffer a competitive disadvantage as compared with undertakings established in Member States that have not eliminated discrimination against female workers as regards pay'.

13 Case 43/75 [1976] ECR 455. This was emphasised in Case C-50/96 *Deutsche Telekom* v. *Schröder* [2000] ECR I-743, paras. 53–5.

> the principle of equal pay suffer a competitive disadvantage in intra-Community competition as compared with undertakings established in states which have not yet eliminated discrimination against women workers as regards pay.

However, having recognised the economic purpose of Article 141, the Court then continued that this provision forms part of the social objectives of the Community, which is not merely an economic union, but is at the same time intended, by common action to ensure social progress and seek the constant improvement of living and working conditions of their peoples. Thus, it was the Court that recognised the 'social' dimension of the social policy provisions, in a way that the original Treaty drafters did not, and the Court has since played a key role not only in fleshing out the meaning of the social policy provisions but also trying to reconcile the social with the economic aspect of the Community.

3. THE WORLDS COLLIDE

As we have seen, social policy was seen to be a national matter and, in the early days of the EU, national social policy, and employment laws in particular, looked like they would not be much affected by the Treaty provisions on persons and services. This is because the Treaty provisions appeared to be underpinned by a non-discrimination model[14] and the Court interpreted the Treaty provisions accordingly. This meant that if national employment laws applied equally to nationals and migrants alike, they would be lawful since they did not discriminate on the grounds of nationality in any way.[15] Therefore a rule on the national minimum wage would be lawful if it applied equally to national and migrant workers alike. If, on the other hand, the Court found the national employment laws to be discriminatory, either directly[16] or indirectly[17], the discriminatory element of the rule would have to be removed but the substance of the law itself

---

14 Article 39(2) provides that freedom of movement of workers 'shall entail the abolition of any discrimination based on nationality between workers of the Member States'; Article 43(2) also provides that 'Freedom of Establishment shall include the right to take up and pursue activities as self-employed persons and to set up and manage undertakings, in particular companies or firms, ..., under the conditions laid down for its own nationals by the law of the country where such establishment is effected, ...'; and Article 50(2) provides that the person providing a service may, in order to do so, temporarily pursue his activity in the state where the service is provided, under the same conditions as are imposed by the State on its own nationals'.

15 See, by analogy, Case 221/85 *Commission* v. *Belgium* [1987] ECR 719; Case 52/79 *Debauve* [1981] ECR 833.

16 Case C-415/93 *Union Royale Belge de Société de Football Association* v. *Bosman* [1995] ECR I-4921.

17 See e.g. Case C-175/88 *Biehl* v. *Administration des Contributions* [1990] ECR I-1779; Case C-111/91 *Commission* v. *Luxembourg* [1993] ECR I-817.

remained in tact.[18] Therefore, a rule which said there could be no more than 5 foreign players in a football team is discriminatory. The discriminatory element of the rule would have to be removed (5 foreign players) but states/football associations remain free to regulate the total number of players in a football team.

While the non-discrimination model left national regulatory autonomy broadly intact, the gradual adoption of the 'restrictions' or 'obstacles' approach, sometimes referred to as the 'market access' approach, changed all this. This change was signalled by *Säger*,[19] in the context of services, where the Court said that Article 49 required:

> *not only* the elimination of all discrimination against a person providing services on the ground of his nationality *but also* the abolition of any restriction, even if it applies without distinction to national providers of services and to those of other Member States, when *it is liable to prohibit or otherwise impede* the activities of a provider of services established in another Member State where he lawfully provides similar services.[20]

The Court continued that any such restriction could be justified by imperative reasons relating to the public interest,[21] provided the measures were proportionate.

The 'restrictions' approach is effective for creating a single market because it removes unjustified barriers to movement. However, it is damaging to national regulatory autonomy because it focuses only on the (potential) effect of the rule on the out-of-state provider. It takes no account of the fact that the domestic provider is also subject to the same rule. This is particularly relevant in the employment context because, under the restrictions model, it could be argued that subjecting any out-of-state service provider (and their staff) to the employment laws of the host state creates an impediment to free movement, regardless of the fact that domestic providers find themselves in the same position. Use of the restrictions approach can be seen in *Commission* v. *France (performing artists)*[22], where the Court said that French law which presumed artists had 'salaried status', resulting in them being subject to the social security scheme for employed workers, constituted a restriction on freedom to provide services. It said that the French system was 'likely both to discourage the artists in question from providing their services in France and discourage French organisers of events from engaging

---

18 See also Article 7(1) of Reg. 1612/68.

19 Case C-76/90 [1991] ECR I-4221, para. 12, emphasis added.

20 Case C-19/92 *Kraus* [1993] ECR I-1663, para. 32 '*liable to hamper or to render less attractive* the exercise by Community nationals, including those of the Member State which enacted the measure, of *fundamental freedoms* guaranteed by the Treaty'.

21 Para. 15.

22 Case C-255/04 *Commission* v. *France (performing artists)* [2006] ECR I-5251, para. 38.

such artists'.[23] The rules therefore breached Article 49. The French government justified its rule on the grounds of social protection of performing artists and the campaign against concealed employment. On the facts the Court found neither justification to be made out.

There is certainly an argument that the *Säger* market access approach can be justified in the field of services because services differ from establishment and workers. As the Court noted in *Säger*[24] itself, a 'Member State may not make the provision of services in its territory subject to compliance with all the conditions required for establishment and thereby deprive of all practical effectiveness the provisions of the Treaty whose object is, precisely, to guarantee the freedom to provide services'. Therefore it was inappropriate to apply the full gamut of national rules to a service provider as to a person seeking to establish themselves or work on a permanent basis in the host state. This would tend to suggest that the non-discrimination model should apply to free movement of workers and freedom of establishment but a restrictions model to services.[25] This approach would coincide with the idea that the principal regulator for goods and services is the home state; any additional restrictions raised by the host state would therefore have to be justified since they interfere with market access. By contrast, in the case of workers and establishment, the principal regulator is the host state and it would seem legitimate for that state to treat migrants in the same way as nationals. Therefore the discrimination model should apply: only if the national rules are directly or unjustifiably indirectly discriminatory should they breach Community law.

However, increasingly the Court has applied the market access approach more widely, making it clear that it was no longer confined to the services cases. For example, in *Commission* v. *Denmark (company vehicles)*,[26] a case concerning the free movement of workers, the Court said:

> It is settled case law that Article 39 EC prohibits not only all discrimination, direct or indirect, based on nationality, but also national rules which are applicable irrespective of the nationality of the workers concerned but impede their freedom of movement.

---

23 Para. 38.

24 Case C-76/90 [1991] ECR I-4221, para. 13. See also Case 33/74 *Van Binsbergen* [1974] ECR 1299, para. 11; Case 205/84 *Commission* v. *Germany (the insurance cases)* [1986] ECR 3755, para. 26, and Case C-484/93 *Svensson* [1995] ECR I-3955; Case C-118/96 *Safir* [1998] ECR I-1897, para. 30.

25 L.Daniele, 'Non-discriminatory Restrictions to the Free Movement of Persons' (1997) 22 *ELRev.* 191.

26 Case C-464/02 *Commission* v. *Denmark (company vehicles)* [2005] ECR I-7929, para. 45. See also Case C-190/98 *Graf* v. *Filzmoser Maschinenbau GmbH* [2000] ECR I-493, para. 18; Case C-387/01 *Weigel* v. *Finanzlandes direction für Vorarlberg* [2004] ECR I-4981, para. 51.

The Court has also regularly applied the restrictions approach to freedom of establishment. This can be seen in *Gebhard*[27] which concerned a German national authorized to practise as a '*Rechtsanwalt*' in Germany who opened chambers in Milan, where he described himself as '*avvocato*' without previously having registered with the Milan Bar as required by national law. The Milan bar objected to this; he argued the Italian rules breached Article 43. The Court said that 'national measures liable to hinder or make less attractive the exercise of fundamental freedoms' breached Article 43,[28] unless they could be justified by the general good, such as for reasons relating to organisation, qualifications, professional ethics, supervision, and liability.[29]

The effect of this shift towards a market access approach is for closer scrutiny of national laws by the European Court of Justice. It has also meant that the Court has had to expand significantly on the relatively short group of justifications which it listed in *Gouda*.[30] For our purposes the most important justifications recognised by the Court are:

- protection of workers.[31] This is sometimes referred to as reasons of social welfare;[32]
- prevention of social dumping[33] or unfair competition;[34]
- avoiding disturbances on the labour market.[35]

The market access approach has also paved the way for lawyers to run ingenious – and, at times, far-fetched arguments – that by being subject to the host state employment laws, migrant workers lose their competitive advantage (eg being willing to work for less than the minimum wage of the host state[36]). It also risks leading to arguments by businesses wishing to set up branches or agencies in another Member State that the fact that they are obliged to comply with the host state's employment laws when employing staff in that state (especially if the host state requires higher

27 Case C-55/94 [1995] ECR I-4165.
28 Para. 37.
29 Para. 35.
30 Case C-288/89 *Stichting Collectieve Antennevoorziening Gouda* v. *Commissariaat voor de Media* [1991] ECR I-4007.
31 Case 279/80 *Webb* [1981] ECR 3305, para. 19; Joined Cases 62–63/81 *Seco* v. *EVI* [1982] ECR 223, para. 14; Case C-113/89 *Rush Portuguesa* [1990] ECR I-1417, para. 18. Subsequently in Case C-272/94 *Guiot* [1996] ECR I-1905, para. 16, the Court stressed the importance of the social protection of workers in the construction industry; Case C-79/01 *Payroll Data Services (Italy)* [2002] ECR I-8923, para. 31.
32 Case C-445/03 *Commission* v. *Luxembourg* [2004] ECR I-10191, para. 28.
33 Case C-244/04 *Commission* v. *Germany* [2006] ECR I-000, para. 61.
34 Case C-60/03 *Wolff & Müller* v. *Pereira Félix* [2004] ECR I-9553, para. 41.
35 Case C-445/03 *Commission* v. *Luxembourg* [2004] ECR I-10191, para. 38.
36 An argument that the ECJ expressly rejected in Case 167/73 *Commission* v. *France* [1974] ECR 359, paras 44–45.

levels of employment protection than in the home state) is liable to restrict their willingness to establish themselves under Article 43. The non-discrimination model would put a stop to such arguments; the market access approach, especially in the absence of a *de minimis* rule, creates a field day for lawyers.

For a number of years, similar arguments were successfully run in the field of taxation: differences in tax rates or the basis of taxation was liable to discourage freedom of establishment. For example, in *Bosal*[37] the Court said that as a result of the national tax rules 'a parent company *might be dissuaded* from carrying on its activities through the intermediary of a subsidiary established in another Member State'[38] and so the rule breached Article 43. This caused consternation among the Member States, who also found the justifications they put forward were being rejected by the Court, with the result that the whole balance in their taxation systems was being called into question. Eventually the Court reverted to a non-discrimination model in the field of taxation.[39]

The Court has not proceeded down this route in the employment sphere. Generally it has continued to deploy the market access approach, as we saw in the *Performing artists* case, combined with justification. However, it has, in certain cases, used a number of other techniques to address the potential conflict between national employment law and Community law on the free movement. We consider these tools in the next section.

4. TOOLS TO ADDRESS THE PROBLEM

When the Court sees a problem of conflict between national employment law and Community law, it can take a number of steps to avoid addressing the problem head on. However, this depends on it seeing the problem.

4.1. WHAT PROBLEM?

In some case the Court cannot see the problem of a potential conflict between EC single market and competition rules and national employment law and policy. For example, in *Macrotron*[40] the Court held that the German Federal Employment

---

37 Case C-168/01 *Bosal Holding BV* v. *Staatssecretaris van Financiën* [2003] ECR I-9409. See also C-9/02 *de Lasteyrie du Saillant* [2004] ECR I-2409, para. 43 'a restriction on freedom of establishment is prohibited by Article [43] of the Treaty even if of limited scope or minor importance'.

38 Para. 27, emphasis added.

39 Joined Cases C-544/03 and C-545/03 *Mobistar SA* v. *Commune de Fleron* [2005] ECR I-7723.

40 Case C-41/90 *Höfner and Elser* v. *Macroton* [1991] ECR I-1979. See also Case C-55/96 *Non-Contentious Proceedings brought by Job Centre Coop arl* [1997] ECR I-7140. See generally, Ricci,

Office (FEO) was not entitled to maintain its statutory monopoly over employment placement services. The Court said the FEO was abusing its dominant position, contrary to Articles 82 and 86, because the statutory service could not meet demand and tolerated private head-hunters, even though their activities were illegal. However, the Court made no reference to the social interest behind the existing legislation: that private employment agencies might be tempted to concentrate on the most attractive job seekers, leaving aside the weaker prospects.[41]

Similarly, in *Porto di Genoa*[42] the Court said that Article 86 precluded national rules which confer on an undertaking established in that state (but not individual dockers)[43] the exclusive right to organise dock work and required it to have recourse to a dock work company formed exclusively of national workers. Although the facts of *Porto di Genoa* were exceptional (the company was abusing its monopoly to demand payment for unrequested services, to offer selective reductions in prices and by refusing to have recourse to modern technology), the most striking feature of the Court's judgment, as Deakin points out,[44] was the almost complete disregard shown for social arguments which could have been made in favour of the dock labour monopoly. In particular, no reference was made to the need to combat casualization of labour.

Commission v. *France*[45] highlighted the potentially damaging scope of the state aid rules to the integrity of national social legislation. The case concerned a decision by the Commission that the financial participation of the French Fonds National de l'emploi (FNE), a state body, in paying for measures included in the social plan drawn up by a company faced with large scale redundancies, constituted a state aid contrary to Article 87(1) and therefore had to be notified to the

---

'Il controverso rapporto fra principi comunitari della concorrenza e normative nazionali del lavoro il caso *Job Centre II*' (1998) 2 *Diritto delle relazioni industriali* 145.

41 S. Sciarra, 'Part II: *Job Centre*: An Illustrative Example of Strategic Litigation', in Sciarra (ed), *Labour Law in the Courts: National Judges and the European Court of Justice* (Hart, Oxford, 2001) 245.

42 Case C-179/90 *Merci Convenzionali Porto di Genova* v. *Siderurgica Gabrielli* [1991] ECR I-5889. See also Case C-163/96 *Criminal Proceedings against Silvano Raso* [1998] ECR I-533; Decision of the Commission 97/744/EC *Re Italian Ports Employment Policy: The Community* v. *Italy* [1998] 4 CMLR 73.

43 Case C-22/98 *Criminal Proceedings against Bew, Verweire, Smeg and Adia Interim* [1999] ECR I-5665.

44 S. Deakin, 'Labour Law as Market Regulation: the Economic Foundations of European Social Policy' in Davies, Lyon-Caen, Sciarra and Simitis (eds), *European Community Labour Law: Principles and Perspectives: Liber Amicorum Lord Wedderburn of Charlton* (Oxford, OUP, 1996), 75.

45 Case C-241/94 *French Republic* v. *Commission* [1996] ECR I-4551. See also Case C-256/97 *Proceedings relating to DMT* [1999] ECR I-3913. See Barnard and Deakin, 'European Community Social Policy: Progression or Regression?' (1998/1999) 2 *IRJ* 117.

Commission.[46] The French government challenged the Commission's initial finding that the payment by FNE came under Article 87 at all, because, if correct, it meant that France would have to notify all similar payments in future to the Commission. The Commission would then have the power to nullify them if the payments did not, in its view (subject to review by the Court), fall under the relevant derogation. The pre-existing case law drew a distinction between measures of general application, which were not aid, and subsidies payable to particular undertakings, which were. The Court said that since the French legislation gave the administration some discretion in the amounts of subsidy which it could grant to a particular employer, this constituted a state aid and so it had to be notified and approved.

It may be that, because these cases were argued by competition lawyers, rather than labour lawyers, the Court was not clearly presented with the implications of its decisions for national employment law. However, when these consequences are presented to it, it is willing to respond and has done so in a variety of ways. Perhaps its most radical conclusion is that the particular area of national social policy remains outside the scope of Community law.

4.2. OUTSIDE THE SCOPE

4.2.1. Albany

Albany[47] is perhaps the best example of the Court removing aspects of social policy from the reach of Community law. The case concerned a collective agreement negotiated by representative organisations of employers and workers setting up a supplementary pension scheme, managed by a pension fund, to which affiliation was compulsory. The Dutch Minister of Employment had, on request of the Social Partners, made affiliation to the scheme compulsory for all workers in the sector. Albany argued that the request by management and labour to make affiliation to a sectoral pension fund compulsory constituted an agreement between the undertakings operating in the sector concerned, contrary to Article 81(1) of the Treaty. It said such an agreement restricted competition because, by

[46] The Commission did, however, conclude that, in the event, the aid was legitimate, since it fell under an exception provided by Article 87(3)(c) which allows aid where it is made 'to facilitate the development of certain economic activities or of certain economic areas, where such aid does not adversely affect trading conditions to an extent contrary to the common interest'. See also Case 203/82 *Commission* v. *Italy* [1983] ECR 2525: legislation reducing employer's sickness insurance contributions by different amounts in respect of male and female employees indirectly benefited certain sectors with more female employees and was declared contrary to Article 87.

[47] Case C-67/96 *Albany International* v. *Stichting Bedrijfspensioenfonds Textielindustrie* [1999] ECR I-5751.

entrusting the operation of a compulsory scheme to a single manager, the agreement deprived the undertakings of affiliating to another pension scheme managed by other insurers and so excluded other insurers from a substantial part of the pension insurance market.

The Court disagreed with Albany. It turned first to the question of principle. It recognised that certain restrictions of competition were inherent in collective agreements between organisations representing employers and workers. However, it said that 'the social policy objectives pursued by such agreements would be seriously undermined if management and labour were subject to Article [81(1)] of the Treaty when seeking jointly to adopt measures to improve conditions of work and employment'.[48] It continued that agreements concluded in the context of collective negotiations between management and labour in pursuit of such objectives had, by virtue of their nature and purpose, to be regarded as falling outside the scope of Article 81(1) of the Treaty.

The Court then considered whether the nature and purpose of the agreement at issue in this case justified its exclusion from Article 81. The Court concluded that it did. It said that the agreement was concluded in the form of a collective agreement and was the outcome of collective negotiations between organisations representing employers and workers. Further, the agreement established, in a given sector, a supplementary pension scheme managed by a pension fund to which affiliation might be made compulsory. The scheme sought generally to guarantee a certain level of pension for all workers in that sector and therefore contributed directly to improving one of their working conditions, namely their remuneration. Thus Article 81 did not apply.[49]

Similarly, in *Van der Woude*[50] the Court said that a collective agreement establishing a health care insurance scheme contributed to improving the working conditions of employees, not only by ensuring that they had the necessary means to meet medical expenses but also by reducing the costs which, in the absence of a collective agreement, would have to be borne by the employees.[51] By reason of its nature and purpose, the agreement did not therefore fall within the scope of Article 81(1).[52]

---

48 Para. 59.

49 Paras. 63–4. See also Joined Cases C-115–7/97 *Brentjens Handelsonderneming BV* v. *Stichting Bedrijfspensioenfonds voor de Handel in Bouwmaterialen* [1999] ECR I-6025; Case C-219/97 *Maatschappij Drijvende Bokken BV* v. *Stichting Pensioenfonds voor de Vervoer- en Havenbedrijven* [1999] ECR I-6121. These cases are considered by Vousden, '*Albany*, Market Law and Social Exclusion' (2000) 29 *ILJ* 181.

50 See also Case C-222/98 *Van der Woude* v. *Stichting Beatrixoord* [2000] ECR I-7111 considered by Evju, 'Collective Agreements and Competition Law. The *Albany* puzzle and *Van der Woude*' (2001) 17 *IJCLLIR* 165.

51 Para. 25.

52 Para. 26.

4.2.2. *The Services Directive*

The Services Directive 2006/123[53] used a similar exclusionary technique to protect labour law from the potential effect of the Directive.[54] It will be recalled that the trade unions were up in arms against the original 2004 'Bolkestein' draft which was perceived as paving the way for social dumping.[55] The issues were particularly sensitive in France, where the 'Polish plumber' had, for many French people, assumed 'bogeyman status as low cost, low standard, Eastern European Labour'.[56] The fear was that the Directive would serve only to exacerbate this, leading to the demise of the European Social Model. After extensive lobbying by the trade union movement, the European Parliament was persuaded to exclude labour law and fundamental rights from its version of the Directive. This was followed by the Commission in its 2006 McCreevy draft which, in turn, was eventually adopted as Directive 2006/123.[57] Article 1(6) provides:

> This Directive *does not affect* labour law, that is any legal or contractual provision concerning employment conditions, working conditions, *including* health and safety at work and the relationship between employers and workers, which Member States apply in accordance with national law which respects Community law. Equally, this Directive does not affect the social security legislation of the Member States.[58]

The deliberately wide drafting of Article 1(6) was intended to make sure that the Directive is 'labour law neutral',[59] a point confirmed by Commissioner McCreevy before the European Parliament:[60]

---

53 OJ [2006] L376/26.

54 See Hendrickx, 'The Services Directive and Social Dumping: National Labour Law under Strain' in Neergaard, Nielsen and Roseberry (eds), *The Services Directive – Consequences for the Welfare State an the European Social Model* (DJØF Publishing, Copenhagen, 2008).

55 COM(2004) 2 final/3. For a full discussion, see Barnard, 'Unravelling the Services Directive' (2008) *CMLRev.* 323.

56 Waterfield, 'Polish workers protest against French bosses' *EUPolitix.com*, 4 October 2005, 1. France was not alone. The Swedish trade minister, Thomas Ostros, was reported as saying 'There cannot be a service directive, unless there is also a protection against social dumping': Küchler, 'McCreevy locks horns with Swedish unions' *euobserver.com*, 10 October 2005. See also Flower, 'Negotiating the Services Directive' (2006–7) 9 *CYELS* 217, 224.

57 See further Barnard, 'Employment Law, the EC Treaty and the Services Directive' in: Rönnmar (ed), *National Industrial Relations vs EC Industrial Relations* (Kluwer, 2008).

58 Emphasis added. In the absence of a Community definition of labour law, the Directive tries to provide some guidance. The protection of discrimination law is mentioned only in the Preamble: 11th Recital. Further details as to what constitutes terms and conditions of employment can be found in the 3th and, more specifically, the 14th Recitals. The 14th Recital explicitly identifies 'the right to strike and to take industrial action in accordance with national law and practices which respect Community law'.

59 Evidence given by Rt Hon Ian McCartney to the House of Lords EU Select Committee on 17 May 2006, annexed to the House of Lords Select Committee 38th Report 2005–6, p.23.

60 SPEEC/06/687, European Parliament Plenary Session, Strasbourg, 15 November 2006.

> The Commission wants to state unambiguously that the Services Directive does indeed not affect labour law laid down in national legislation and established practices in the Member States and that it does not affect collective rights which the social partners enjoy according to national legislation and practices.

Article 1(7) adopted of the Directive applied a similar approach to fundamental rights, making clear that the Directive did 'not affect' the exercise of fundamental rights as recognised in the Member States and by Community law. It continued 'Nor does it affect the right to negotiate, conclude and enforce collective agreements and to take industrial action in accordance with national law and practices which respect Community law'.[61] As we shall see, the effectiveness of this exclusion has been undermined by the decision in *Laval*.

4.2.3. The Solidarity Principle

In respect of social welfare schemes the Court has used the solidarity principle to protect certain social welfare schemes from the ravages of EC competition law:[62] the Court says that where the activity is based on national solidarity, it is not an economic activity and therefore the body concerned cannot be classed as an undertaking to which Articles 81 and 82 apply. This principle, when applied, indicates a certain supremacy for social protection over the Single Market.

The principle was first recognised in this context in *Poucet and Pistre*[63] where the Court held that certain French bodies administering the sickness and maternity insurance scheme for self-employed persons engaged in non-agricultural occupations and the basic pension scheme for skilled trades, were not to be classified as undertakings for the purpose of competition law. The schemes provided a basic pension.[64] Affiliation was compulsory. The schemes operated on a redistributive basis with active members' contributions being directly used to finance the pensions of retired members. The scheme had a social objective in that it was intended to provide cover for the beneficiaries against the risks of sickness or old age regardless of the individuals' financial status and state of health at the time of affiliation. The principle of solidarity was embodied in the *redistributive* nature of the pension scheme: contributions paid by active workers served to finance the pensions of retired workers. It was also reflected by the grant of

61 See also the 15th Recital, which expressly refers to the Charter and the accompanying explanations.

62 For a fuller consideration of these developments, see Barnard, 'Solidarity and New Governance in the Field of Social Policy' in De Búrca and Scott (eds), *New Governance and Constitutionalism in Europe and the US* (Hart, Oxford, 2006).

63 Joined Cases C-159/91 and C-160/91 *Poucet and Pistre* v. *AGF and Cancava* [1993] ECR I-637.

64 These are helpfully summarised by Advocate General Jacobs in his Opinion in Case C-67/96 *Albany* [1999] ECR I-5751, para. 317.

pension rights where no contributions had been made and of pension rights that were not proportional to the contributions paid. Finally, there was solidarity between the various social security schemes, with those in surplus contributing to the financing of those with structural difficulties. The Court therefore said:

> It follows that the social security schemes, as described, are based on a system of compulsory contribution, which is indispensable for the application of the principle of solidarity and the financial equilibrium of those schemes.
> ... [O]rganisations involved in the management of the public social security system fulfil an exclusively social function. That activity is based on the principle of national solidarity and is entirely non-profit-making. The benefits paid are statutory benefits bearing no relation to the amount of the contribution. Accordingly, that activity is not an economic activity...

However, in *FFSA*[65] the Court 'clarified' its case law. The case concerned a French supplementary retirement scheme for self-employed farmers.[66] The Court noted that in *FFSA* membership of the scheme was optional, that the scheme operated in accordance with the principle of capitalization, rather than on a redistributive basis as in *Poucet*, and that the benefits to which it conferred entitlement depended solely on the amount of contributions paid by the recipients and the financial results of the investments made by the managing organisation. It concluded that the managing body therefore carried on an economic activity in competition with life assurance companies and so the Community competition rules, in particular Article 81, applied. On the question of solidarity the Court said that 'the principle of solidarity is extremely limited in scope' and noted that while the scheme had solidaristic elements that was not sufficient to take the scheme outside Article 81.

Although the Court's initial enthusiasm for the principle of solidarity seemed to have rather cooled after *FFSA*, the principle was successfully invoked in *Sodemare*[67] to allow Italy to insist that only non-profit-making private operators could participate in the running of its social welfare system. The Italian rules did not breach Articles 43 and 48 because, as the Court noted, the system of social welfare, whose implementation is in principle entrusted to the public authorities, is based on the principle of solidarity, as reflected by the fact that it is designed as a matter of priority to assist those who are in a state of need.[68]

---

65 Case C-244/94 *Fédération Française des Sociététs d'Assurances* [1995] ECR I-4013 discussed by Laigre, 'L'intrusion du droit communautaire de la concurrence dans le champ de la protection sociale' [1996] *Droit Social* 82.

66 Case C-67/96 *Albany* v. *Stichting Bedrijfspensioenfonds Textielindustrie* [1999] ECR I-5751, para. 325.

67 Case C-70/95 *Sodemare* v. *Regione Lombardia* [1997] ECR I-3395.

68 Para. 29.

Since *Sodemare* the Court has carefully examined the facts of the individual cases to consider whether there is a sufficient degree of solidarity to justify a finding that the activity is not economic, so falling outside the scope of Community law or insufficient solidarity and so Community law applies. For example, in *AOK*[69] the Court found that the sickness funds in the German statutory health insurance scheme were involved in the management of the social security system where they fulfilled 'an exclusively social function which is founded on the principle of national solidarity and is entirely non-profit-making'.[70] Since the funds were obliged by law to offer their members essentially identical benefits, irrespective of contributions, that they were bound together in a type of community founded on the basis of solidarity which enabled an equalization of costs and risks between them and they did not compete with one another or private institutions,[71] the Court considered they fell on the *Poucet and Pistre* side of the line and so their activity could not be regarded as economic in nature. On the other hand, in *Wouters*[72] the Court said that because a professional regulatory body such as the Bar of the Netherlands was neither fulfilling a social function based on the principle of solidarity nor exercising powers which were typically those of a public authority, it did engage in an economic activity and so was subject to Community law.

69 Joined Cases C-264/01, C-306/01, C-354/01 and C-355/01 *AOK Bundesverband, Bundesverband der Betriebskrankenkassen (BKK), Bundesverband der Innungskrankenkassen, Bundesverband der landwirtschaftlichen Krankenkassen, Verband der Angestelltenkrankenkassen eV, Verband der Arbeiter-Ersatzkassen, Bundesknappschaft and See-Krankenkasse* v. *Ichthyol-Gesellschaft Cordes, Hermani & Co. (C-264/01), Mundipharma GmbH (C-306/01), Gödecke GmbH (C-354/01) and Intersan, Institut für pharmazeutische und klinische Forschung GmbH (C-355/01)* [2004] ECR I-000. See also Case C-218/00 *Cisal di Battistello Venanzio & C.Sas* v. *Istituto nazionale per l'assicurazione contro gli infortuni sul lavoro* [2002] ECR I-691 concerning compulsory insurance against accidents at work and occupational diseases; Case C-355/00 *Freskot AE* v. *Elliniko Dimosio* [2003] ECR I-5263; Case T-319/99 *FENIN* v. *Commission* [2003] ECR II-357 concerning the bodies which run the Spanish national health system); Joined Cases C-266/04 to C-270/04 *Nazairdis* v. *Caisse nationale de l'orgaisation autonome d'assurance viellesse des travailleurs non salariés des professions industrielles et commerciales (Organic)* [2005] ECR I-000, para. 54 (old age insurance schemes for self employed persons in the craft sector). See Sciarra, 'Market Freedom and fundamental social rights' in Hepple (ed), *Social and Labour Rights in a Global Context* (CUP, Cambridge, 2002).

70 Para. 51.

71 Paras. 51–3.

72 Case C-309/99 *Wouters, Savelbergh, Price Waterhouse Belastingadviseurs* BV v. *Algemene Raad van de Nederlandse Orde van* Advocaten [2002] ECR I-1577, para. 58. See also Case C-55/96 *Job Centre Coop. Arl* [1997] ECR I-7119.

4.3. REMOTENESS/NO SUBSTANTIAL HINDRANCE OF MARKET ACCESS

So far we have considered attempts to ringfence aspects of social policy from the scope of EC law. In other cases the Court (instinctively?) felt that the *Säger* restrictions model was going too far and so found no breach of the Treaty. So in *Burbaud*[73] the Court said that the requirement of passing an exam in order to take up a post in the public service could not 'in itself be regarded as an obstacle' to free movement.[74] A similar approach can be seen in *Deliège*.[75] A successful Belgian judo player complained that the Belgian judo federation's failure to select her for various international competitions breached Article 49. The Court disagreed, saying that, although selection rules inevitably had the effect of limiting the number of participants in a tournament, such a limitation was inherent in the conduct of an international high-level sports event. In other words, without any rules there would be no competition. The Court continued that such rules could not in themselves be regarded as constituting a restriction on the freedom to provide services prohibited by Article 49.[76]

Perhaps, most significantly, the Court recognised in *Graf*[77] that there were limits to the market access approach. Graf, a German national, worked for his Austrian employer for four years when he terminated his contract in order to take up employment in Germany. Under Austrian law, a worker employed by the same employer for more than three years was entitled to a termination payment provided that he was dismissed (and did not just resign). Graf argued that this law contravened Article 39 because the effect of the rule was that, by moving to another State, he lost the chance of being dismissed in Austria and so was unable to claim compensation.

The Court disagreed: the Austrian law was genuinely non-discriminatory and did not preclude or deter a worker from ending his contract of employment in order to take a job with another employer.[78] The Court explained that the entitlement to the termination payment was not dependent on the worker's choosing whether or not to stay with his current employer but on a future and hypothetical event (being dismissed).[79] The Court concluded that '[s]uch an event is *too uncertain and indirect* a possibility for legislation to be capable of being

73 Case C-285/01 *Isabel Burbaud* v. *Ministère de l'Emploi et de la Solidarité* [2003] ECR.
74 Para. 96. To emphasise the point, the Court said that inasmuch as all new jobs are subject to a recruitment procedure, the requirement of passing a recruitment competition could not 'in itself be liable to dissuade candidates who have already sat a similar competition in another Member State from exercising their right to freedom of movement as workers' (para. 97).
75 Joined Cases C-51/96 & C-191/97 *Deliège* [2000] ECR I-2549, para. 64.
76 Para. 64.
77 Case C-190/98 *Graf* v. *Filzmozer Maschinenbau GmbH* [2000] ECR I-493.
78 Para. 23.
79 Para. 24.

regarded as liable to hinder free movement for workers'. Thus, in *Graf* the Court says that the event was too remote to be considered liable to affect free movement.[80] Putting it another way using economic rather than tortious, causation-based language, non-discriminatory measures which do not substantially hinder access to the (labour) market,[81] or whose effect on free movement is too remote, fall outside Article 39.[82]

4.4. FINDING A BREACH BUT LOOKING AT JUSTIFICATIONS AND PROPORTIONALITY

In the cases we have considered so far, the Court has found ways to establish that the national rules do not breach Community law. However, increasingly the Court has applied the market access approach to such cases (looking for a restriction, finding a breach, justifying the breach and proportionality). This is increasingly the most common approach to cases involving a conflict between national employment laws and free movement and, once applied, the Court quite often finds national employment laws incompatible with EC law. This can best be illustrated by some of the cases on posting of workers. For example, *Mazzoleni*[83] concerned a French company, ISA, which provided security guards who worked on a part-time basis for brief periods at a shopping mall in Belgium. In the course of an inspection by the Belgian labour inspectorate, it was found that the monthly wage of ISA workers was less than the minimum wage in Belgium, albeit that their remuneration package as a whole, including tax and social security contributions was similar to, if not more favourable than, remuneration under Belgian law. The Court said that the Belgian law breached Article 49 because, by subjecting service providers to all conditions required for establishment, it deprived the provisions on services of practical effectiveness. However, it said the requirement to pay the host state's minimum wage could be justified on the grounds of worker protection, although it concluded by suggesting that the

80 See also Joined Cases C-418/93, C-419/93, C-420/93, C-421/93, C-460/93, C-461/93, C-462/93, C-464/93, C-9/94, C-10/94, C-11/94, C-14/94, C-15/94 *Semeraro Casa Uno Srl and others* [1996] ECR I-2975, para. 32 concerning Article 43. *Cf.* Case C-159/90 *SPUC* v. *Grogan* [1991] ECR I-4685, para. 24, where the Court noted that the link between the student associations and abortions carried out by clinics in other Member States was 'too tenuous' for the prohibition on the distribution of information to be regarded as a restriction within the meaning of Article 49; Case C-168/91 *Konstantinidis* [1993] ECR I-1191, para. 15.

81 Case C-190/98 *Graf*, above nr. 77, para. 23.

82 See also Case C-134/03 *Viacom Outdoor Srl* v. *Giotto Immobilier SARL (Viacom II)* [2005] ECR I-1167, para. 38.

83 Case C-165/98 *Criminal proceedings against André Mazzoleni and Inter Surveillance Assistance SARL* [2001] ECR I-2189.

application of the Belgian rules might be disproportionate.[84] It said that the Belgian objective of worker protection would be attained if all the workers concerned enjoyed an equivalent position overall in relation to remuneration, taxation and social security contributions in the host Member State and in the Member State of establishment.[85] It continued that the application of Belgian law on minimum wages to service providers established in a frontier region of a Member State could result, first, in an additional, disproportionate administrative burden including, in certain cases, the calculation, hour-by-hour, of the appropriate remuneration for each employee according to whether he has, in the course of his work, crossed the frontier of another Member State and, second, in the payment of different levels of wages to employees who were all attached to the same operational base and carried out identical work. That last consequence might, in its turn, result in tension between employees and even threaten the cohesion of the collective labour agreements that are applicable in the Member State of establishment.[86]

It is this same market access approach which structured the Court's decisions in *Viking* and *Laval*.

5. *VIKING* AND *LAVAL*

5.1. ESTABLISHING BREACH

It will be recalled that *Viking* concerned the selling of a Finnish vessel to an Estonian subsidiary, reflagging the vessel in Estonia and employing an Estonian crew. *Laval* concerned a Latvian company carrying out a building contract in Sweden using Latvian workers and paying them below the Swedish – but not the Latvian – collectively agreed wage rates. In both cases trade unions either threatened (*Viking*) or actually did (*Laval*) take industrial action to stop both situations from occurring. Employers sought to challenge this industrial action – which was legitimate under national law – as being incompatible with Community law.[87]

The trade unions and certain governments argued that the Court should use any one of the tools outlined above to prevent Community law from applying to this case (i.e. by arguing that there is no breach). Their arguments fell on deaf ears. In *Viking* the Court began with the stark statement that collective action falls in

84 Para. 34.

85 Para. 35.

86 Para. 36.

87 A more detailed discussion of these cases can be found in Chapter 3 of this volume. See also Barnard, '*Viking* and *Laval*: An Introduction' (2007–8) *CYELS* 463, from which some of this section draws.

principle 'within the scope of Article 43'.[88] It dismissed the argument that just because Article 137(5) excluded Community competence in respect of, *inter alia*, the right to strike, strike action as a whole fell outside the scope of Community law.[89] The Court also rejected the argument that fundamental rights fell outside Community law. Pointing to *Schmidberger*[90] and *Omega*,[91] the Court noted that in those cases the fundamental rights at issue (freedom of expression and freedom of assembly and respect for human dignity) did not fall outside the scope of the provisions of the Treaty; rather the exercise of fundamental rights had to be reconciled with the requirements relating to rights protected under the Treaty and in accordance with the principle of proportionality.[92] In other words, fundamental rights could be used to justify restrictions on free movement but were not ringfenced from the rules on free movement.[93]

Finally, the Court rejected the argument that the decision in *Albany*[94] should apply by analogy.[95] The Court confined its decision in that case (collectively agreed terms and conditions improving conditions of work and employment fall outside Article 81(1)) to competition cases and refused to extend it to free movement cases.[96] It said 'the fact that an agreement or an activity are excluded from the scope of the provisions of the Treaty on competition does not mean that that agreement or activity also falls outside the scope of the Treaty provisions on the free movement of persons or services since those two sets of provisions are to be applied in different circumstances.[97]

Having rejected all attempts to disapply Community law, the Court adopted the market access approach in its full vigour. First, the Advocate Generals and then the Court concluded that the collective action breached Community law. For example, in *Laval* the Court said:[98]

> ... it must be pointed out that the right of trade unions of a Member State to take collective action by which undertakings established in other Member States may be forced to sign the collective agreement for the building sector – certain terms of which

88 Para.37.
89 Paras. 39–41; *Laval*, para. 88.
90 C-112/00 *Schmidberger* [2003] ECR I-5659, para. 77.
91 Case C-36/02 *Omega* [2004] ECR I-9609, para. 36.
92 Para. 46. *Laval*, para. 94.
93 Para. 45. *Laval*, para. 93.
94 Case C-67/96 *Albany* [1999] ECR I-5751.
95 This point was not discussed at all in *Laval*.
96 *Viking* para. 51.
97 *Viking* para. 53, citing Case C-519/04 P *Meca-Medina and Majcen* v. *Commission* [2006] ECR I-6991. For good measure it cited three cases where the Court had found that the terms of collective agreements were not excluded from the scope of the Treaty provisions on freedom of movement for persons: Case C-15/96 *Schöning-Kougebetopoulou* [1998] ECR I-47; Case C-35/97 *Commission* v. *France* [1998] ECR I-5325; and Case C-400/02 *Merida* [2004] ECR I-8471.
98 Para. 99.

> depart from the legislative provisions and establish more favourable terms and conditions of employment as regards the matters referred to in Article 3(1), first subparagraph, (a) to (g) of Directive 96/71 and others relate to matters not referred to in that provision – is liable to make it less attractive, or more difficult, for such undertakings to carry out construction work in Sweden, and therefore constitutes a restriction on the freedom to provide services within the meaning of Article 49 EC.

Having established a breach, the next question was whether the collective action could be justified and proportionate.

5.2. JUSTIFICATIONS AND PROPORTIONALITY

In both *Viking* and *Laval* the Court began by recognising the need to reconcile the competing objectives of the Community: on the one hand the completion of the internal market and on the other 'a policy in the social sphere'.[99] The Court made the important observation that:

> Since the Community has thus not only an economic but also a social purpose, the rights under the provisions of the Treaty on the free movement of goods, persons, services and capital must be balanced against the objectives pursued by social policy, which include, as is clear from the first paragraph of Article 136 EC, inter alia, improved living and working conditions, so as to make possible their harmonisation while improvement is being maintained, proper social protection and dialogue between management and labour.[100]

These observations are the direct descendant of the Court of Justice's remarks in *Defrenne II*: they show just how far the EU has come from its purely economic origins when merely a European *Economic* Community. They suggest that social policy is no longer residual; it is as important as the economic policies of the Community.[101] This perspective is confirmed by the Lisbon Treaty which talks, in Article 2, of establishing a 'social market economy' as an aim of the European Union.[102] However, the application of the market access approach in this case

---

99 Para. 78; *Laval*, para. 104.

100 Para. 79; *Laval*, para. 105.

101 See also the earlier decision in Joined Cases C-270/97 and C0271/97 *Deutsche Post AG* v. *Elisabeth Sievers and Brunhilde Schrage* [2000] ECR I-929.

102 For a discussion of this term, see Joerges and Rödl, "Social Market Economy" as Europe's Social Model?' EUI Working Paper Law No. 2004/8, 19 who argue that 'this concept contained an ordoliberal basis which was complemented by social and societal policies, whose aims and instruments were supposed to rely on market mechanisms'. See also Joerges, 'Democracy and European Integration: A Legacy of Tensions, a Reconceptualisation and Recent True Conflicts' EUI Working Paper, Law 2007/25.

belies this observation: economic policies take precedence because national employment rules are presumptively unlawful.

The Court then noted in *Viking* that 'the right to take collective action for the protection of workers is a legitimate interest which, in principle, justifies a restriction of one of the fundamental freedoms guaranteed by the Treaty', citing *Schmidberger*, and that 'the protection of workers is one of the overriding reasons of public interest recognised by the Court'.[103] Having recognised these two justifications as potentially valid, the Court then considered whether the objectives pursued by the Finnish Seamen's Union (FSU) and the International Transport Federation (ITF) through collective action did actually concern the protection of workers.[104] Although it said that this assessment was the task of the national court,[105] the Court of Justice gave the national court a very strong steer as to which way it should go. In respect of the collective action taken by the *FSU*, it said:

> even if that action – aimed at protecting the *jobs and conditions of employment* of the members of that union *liable to be adversely affected* by the reflagging of the *Rosella* – could reasonably be considered to fall, at first sight, within the objective of protecting workers, such a view would no longer be tenable if it were established that the jobs or conditions of employment at issue were not jeopardised or under serious threat.[106]

This is the crux of the judgment: collective action can be taken but only to protect both jobs and conditions of employment which are liable to be adversely affected. However, Viking, presumably on good advice, had given an undertaking that neither it, nor the companies within the same group, would 'by reason of the reflagging terminate the employment of any person employed by them (which undertaking did not require the renewal of short term employment contracts or prevent the redeployment of any employee on equivalent terms and conditions)'. This undertaking was expressly referred to by the Court of Appeal of England and Wales in its 10th question to the ECJ. The Court of Justice's response was that the jobs or conditions of employment were not jeopardised or under serious threat 'in particular, if it transpired that the undertaking referred to by the national court in its 10th question was, from a legal point of view, as binding as the terms of a collective agreement and if it was of such a nature as to provide a guarantee to the workers that the statutory provisions would be complied with and the terms of the collective agreement governing their working relationship maintained'.[107] Since the exact legal scope of the undertaking was not clear from the order for

103 Para. 77.
104 Para. 80.
105 Para. 80.
106 Para. 81, emphasis added.
107 Para. 82.

reference, 'it is for the national court to determine whether the jobs or conditions of employment of that trade union's members who are liable to be affected by the reflagging of the *Rosella* were jeopardised or under serious threat.'[108]

The Court then considered the situation were the national court to find that the jobs or conditions of employment of the FSU's members were in fact jeopardised or under serious threat. It said that the national court would have to apply the proportionality test i.e. 'whether the collective action initiated by FSU is suitable for ensuring the achievement of the objective pursued and does not go beyond what is necessary to attain that objective.'[109]

On the question of suitability or 'appropriateness',[110] the Court said that 'it should be borne in mind that it is common ground that collective action, like collective negotiations and collective agreements, may, in the particular circumstances of a case, be one of the main ways in which trade unions protect the interests of their members', citing two ECtHR decisions in support.[111]

On the question of necessity, the Court said 'it is for the national court to examine, in particular, on the one hand, whether, under the national rules and collective agreement law applicable to that action, FSU did not have other means at its disposal which were less restrictive of freedom of establishment in order to bring to a successful conclusion the collective negotiations entered into with Viking, and, on the other, whether that trade union had exhausted those means before initiating such action.'[112] Thus, the Court of Justice appears to suggest that industrial action should be the last resort; and the British courts will have to verify whether the FSU has exhausted all other avenues under Finnish law before the industrial action is found proportionate.

Finally, the Court turned to ITF's situation. The Court was adamant: where the FOC policy resulted in (Finnish) shipowners being prevented from registering their vessels in a State other than that of which the beneficial owners of those vessels are nationals (Estonia), the restrictions on freedom of establishment resulting from such action could not be objectively justified.[113]

The Court's reasoning in *Laval* is considerably more truncated and opaque. It recognised that 'the right to take collective action for the protection of the workers of the host State against possible social dumping may constitute an overriding reason of public interest within the meaning of the case law of the Court which, in principle, justifies a restriction of one of the fundamental freedoms guaranteed

108 Para. 83.
109 Para. 84.
110 Para. 86.
111 *Syndicat national de la police belge* v. *Belgium*, of 27 October 1975, Series A, No 19, and *Wilson, National Union of Journalists and Others* v. *United Kingdom* of 2 July 2002, 2002-V, §44.
112 Para. 87.
113 Para. 88.

by the Treaty'.[114] It then added that 'blockading action by a trade union of the host Member State which is aimed at ensuring that workers posted in the framework of a transnational provision of services have their terms and conditions of employment fixed at a certain level, falls within the objective of protecting workers'.[115] The Court then said that using collective action to secure Laval's signature on the collective agreement could not be justified[116] nor could it be justified for a national system to be so unclear at to what is required of the foreign service provider in terms of pay.[117] Thus, in both *Viking* and *Laval* the Court sent a strong indication to the national court that collective action taken by trade unions contravened Articles 43 and 49 of the Treaty. This belies its observation made early in both judgments that:

> the right to take collective action, including the right to strike, must therefore be recognised as a fundamental right which forms an integral part of the general principles of Community law the observance of which the Court ensures.[118]

Herein lies one of the paradoxes of the *Viking* and *Laval* judgments: cases which, for the first time, give express recognition to the right to strike as a fundamental human right, do not lead to enhanced protection of that right. The Court did say that the right to take industrial action was not absolute but subject to 'certain restrictions': 'As is reaffirmed by Article 28 of the Charter of Fundamental Rights of the European Union, those rights are to be protected in accordance with Community law and national law and practices.'[119] In other words, the right to strike can be limited by national law (such as rules on balloting and notice requirements) *and* Community law, in particular the rules on free movement. And the Community law restrictions are strict: the right to take collective action under Community law is justified only where jobs or conditions of employment are jeopardised or under serious threat, and collective action is the last resort. This decision has implications too for Article 1(7) of the Services Directive and Article 28 of the Charter which also recognises the right to take collective action. Both contain the same caveat that the right is subject to national law and practice *and* Community law. Following *Viking* and *Laval* the Treaty-based Community law limitations essentially circumvent the exception for labour law and fundamental rights carved out by the Services Directive.

---

114 Para. 103.
115 Para. 107.
116 Para. 108.
117 Para. 110.
118 Para. 44. *Laval*, para. 91.
119 Para. 44.

6. CONCLUSIONS

Viking and *Laval* confirm a sea change in approach in the Court's approach to the relationship between the Treaty provisions on free movement and national employment laws. Not only did the Court expressly reject any of the potential tools for avoiding a conflict between the two sets of rules but it applied the market access approach with full rigour, unmitigated by any reference to margin of appreciation.[120] These decisions are bad news for the trade union movement. In transnational disputes, employers will now argue that the tests laid down by the Court in *Viking* and *Laval* have not been satisfied and so will more easily seek interlocutory injunctions. They will argue that there is a possibility of a settlement just round the corner so trade unions have not exhausted all means before taking industrial action.[121]

Trade unions might take some comfort from the fact that each case was distinctive and could be explained on the basis of its facts. To a dispassionate observer, the extent and scope of the industrial action in *Viking*, especially the secondary industrial action,[122] might seem excessive when no job losses were at stake. In *Laval*, the Court clearly took against a number of aspects of the Swedish system, in particular its lack of transparency in respect of pay[123] and the Swedish government's failure to take advantage of the possibilities provided in the Directive for addressing the problem.[124] It also objected to the fact that Laval was 'required' to negotiate with trade unions 'in order to ascertain the wages to be paid to workers and to sign the collective agreement for the building sector';[125] and that these negotiations might be of 'unspecified duration';[126] that the designated liaison office set up under the Posted Workers Directive could not help;[127] nor would the police step into assist Laval since the blockade was lawful under Swedish law.[128] In less exceptional circumstances, the Court might have been more sympathetic. However, these are mere chinks of light for the trade union movement. For so long as the Court continues to apply its market access approach with full vigour to such cases, trade unions and, by implication, national employment laws in the wealthier Northern states will continue to find themselves in a precarious position

120 Cf Case C-250/06 *United Pan-Europe Communications Belgium SA* v. *Etat belge* [2007] ECR I-000.

121 See the Balpa dispute currently occurring in the UK: www.balpa.org.uk/intranet/Media---Pr/BA%20Pilots%20Strike5.htm; *www.balpa.org.uk/Media---Pr/BA%20Pilots%20Strike11.htm.*

122 Although the Court did not declare secondary industrial action invalid in itself.

123 Para. 36 and para. 110.

124 Paras. 67–71.

125 Para. 63. See also para. 71. It also did not like the rigidity of the Swedish system: eg the collective agreement was for an hourly not a monthly rate (para. 25).

126 Para. 100.

127 Para. 35.

128 Para. 34.

in the face of European Community law. Conversely, for the Court its perspective is different. It has essentially endorsed the settlement advocated by Spaak in the early days of the Community: the free movement provisions and principles of comparative advantage are the best way of securing greater prosperity for all: there may be pain in the process of the short-medium term adjustment for Swedish and Finnish workers but Latvian and Estonian workers benefit as a consequence. This may not be popular in the Northern states but it is the price they agreed to pay when they signed the Treaty themselves and agreed to the accession of the EU-10.

THE RIGHT TO TAKE COLLECTIVE ACTION *V.* FUNDAMENTAL ECONOMIC FREEDOMS IN THE AFTERMATH OF *LAVAL* AND *VIKING*

Foes are forever!

Prof. dr. Filip Dorssemont

Promoteur M.I.S. "Mobilité Ulysse" FNRS-FRS
Faculté de Droit – Université Catholique de Louvain

"Le blocage progressif de tous les mécanismes politiques et sociaux susceptibles de métaboliser les ressources de la violence sociale ne pourra bien sûr engendrer à terme que de la violence, mais ce sont les Etats-membres et non les institutions communautaires qui devront y faire face".
A. Supiot

"Free movement of persons and rights of participation and representation such as the freedom of association, the right to collective bargaining, and the right to collective action should be considered as instrumental to a *fully* functioning integrated market which can increase efficiency and wealth maximization".
M.E.P. Maduro

1. INTRODUCTION

Due to preliminary references from the London Court of Appeal and the Stockholm *Arbetsdomstolen* the Court of Justice was obliged to rule on an alleged conflict between fundamental economic freedoms firmly anchored in the TEC and the right to take collective action as protected under Finnish and Swedish domestic law. Both references sprang from cases which were brought to domestic Courts by the employers *Viking Line ABP* and *Laval un Partneri Ltd.* The strategy of both employers was intended to prohibit collective actions *ad futurum* (*Viking)* and to obtain compensation for damages suffered (*Laval)* due to a collective action which had proved to be "successful". Since both collective actions were legitimate under domestic law, the litigation tends to corroborate a pre-existing suspicion that Market Integration can intrude on the protection of labour law standards which are deeply rooted in domestic and international legal orders. Similar kinds of conflicts have occurred in the past. *Viking* and *Laval* have highlighted tensions[1] between Market Integration and the so-called social dimension of the European Union in a more dramatic way. However, the previous cases predate the Maastricht Agreement on Social Policy (1992). The Court now had to rule in an era where the discourse on the Social Dimension has been supplemented by the Newspeak on the European Social Model. The rulings in *Laval* and *Viking* have virtually coincided with a second attempt to integrate the Nice Charter of Fundamental Rights in primary EC Law. In previous cases, some domestic labour standards which were not, or at least not directly, related to fundamental workers' rights have come under attack.[2] There was a momentum and a machinery for a genuine human rights approach. *In casibus*, employers have tried to profit from EC Law to undermine a fundamental workers' right which lies at the heart of the creation of contractual labour standards.

Both pending references have aroused anxiety and concern among academic labour lawyers.[3] However, the submissions in both cases provide evidence of divergent opinions among Member States regarding the relation between the conflicting legal principles. Both judgements have given rise and will give rise to abundant comments.[4]

---

1 See S. Giubboni, *Social Rights and Market Freedoms in the European Union* (Cambridge University Press, Cambridge, 2006).

2 *Cf.* ECJ, C-145/88 (*Torfaen Borough Council* v *B&Q plc*) [1989] ECR 3851(prohibition on Sunday trading); ECJ, C-179/90 (*Merci Convenzionali Porto di Genova* v *Siderurgica Gabrielli*) [1991] ECR I-5889 (the monopoly of Italian dockers); ECJ, C-41/90 (*Höfner and Elser* v *Macrotron GmbH*) [1991] ECR I-1979 (the issue of public job-placement monopolies).

3 For doctrinal comments on the pending references: K. Ahlberg, N. Bruun and J. Malmberg, "The Vaxholm case from a Swedish and European perspective", [2006], *Transfer* 155; T. Blanke, "The Viking case", [2006] *Transfer* 251; B. Bercusson, "Trade Union Movement and the European Union: Judgement Day", [2006] *ELJ*, 279–308; A.C.L. Davies, "The Right to Strike Versus Freedom of Establishment in EC Law: The Battle Commences", [2006] *ILJ*, 75–86; F. Dorssemont and T. Jaspers, "Collectieve actie en vrij verkeer", [2007], *Nieuw Juridisch Weekblad*, 2–14; R. Eklund, "The Laval Case", [2006], *ILJ*, 202–208; A. T.M. Jacobs "Gaan liberale marktprincipes het stakinsgrecht insnoeren?", [2006], *Sociaal Maandblad*,1325–140; T. Novitz, "The right to strike and re-flagging in the European Union: free movement of provisions and human rights", [2006] *LMCLQ*, 242–256.

4 See inter alia: P. Chaumette, "Les actions collectives syndicales dans le maillage des libertés communautaires des enterprises, [2008] *Droit social* 210–220; A.Ph.C.M. Jaspers, "Collectieve actie door vakbonden beperkt wegens strijd met vrijheid van diensten en vestiging", [2008], *Nederlands Tijdschrift voor Sociaal Recht*, 56–60; T. Van Peijpe, "De arresten Laval en Viking en hun gevolgen", [2008], *Sociaal Maandblad Arbeid*, 175–186; N. Reich, "Free Movement v. Social Rights in an Enlarged European Union – the Laval and Viking Case before the ECJ", [2008] *German Law Journal*, 125–160; S. Robin-Olivier and E. Pataut, "Europe sociale ou Europe économique", [2008], *Revue de Droit du Travail*, 80–81 and C. Vigneau, Note, *JCP/La semaine juridique*, [2008], II 1060, 33–36. The European Trade Union Institute has developed

The present contribution does not seek to annotate both judgements. It reflects on the relation between fundamental economic freedoms and the right to take collective action in the aftermath of *Viking* and *Laval*. That relation will be studied on the basis of other relevant instruments of primary and secondary EC law. Both cases will be situated within the case law of the Court of Justice dealing with similar issues such as collective bargaining and with similar actions undertaken by other collective actors.

Some legal issues which lay at the heart of the *Laval* case will be dealt with insofar as they shed some light on this contentious relationship. In *Laval* the issue was raised whether Article 49 and Article 3 of the Posting of Workers Directive preclude a collective action by trade unions to attempt to force a foreign service provider to sign a collective agreement in the host country, if the situation in the host country is such that the legislation to implement Directive 96/71 has no express provisions concerning the application of terms and conditions in collective agreements. Thus, I do not intend to contribute to a better understanding of the scope and meaning of the Posting of Workers Directive in its own right. Instead, the focus will be on the impact of the Freedom to Provide Services, as exemplified and regulated by the Posting of Workers Directive, on the right to have recourse to collective action. In the same vein, the contribution seeks to examine the relevance of both judgements for the right to take collective action in a conceptual way, transcending the more topical issues of its impact on existing Scandinavian systems of industrial relations.

The relation concerned is multifaceted. It focuses on conflicts between the European Union and other legal orders (*i.e.* domestic legal orders and other international legal orders) as well as conflicts between legal precepts of the European Union.

2. THE RIGHT TO TAKE COLLECTIVE ACTION AS A "*DROIT CONTRAIRE AU DROIT*"

The authoritative French lawyer Marcel Planiol has qualified the right to strike as "un droit contraire au droit" (a right which is at odds with the law).[5] A shrewd observer has suggested that collective actions challenge major obligations stemming from contractual, property and tort law. Hence, they are qualified as a

a website with references to doctrine in the Member States related to *Laval* and *Viking*. (www.etui-rehs.org/en/Headline-issues/Viking-Laval-Rueffert/2-Articles-de-la-litterature-academique-sur-les-jugements).

5 M. Planiol, annotation of Cour de Bourges, 19 June 1894, *Dalloz Périodiaue*, II, 441.

legal *Fremdkörper*.[6] The etymology of the French word for strike (*grève*) refers to the idea of (collectively) not performing work due under an employment contract. In principle it violates the rule of "Pacta sunt servanda".[7] It generates contractual liability on behalf of the employees on strike. Trade unions *actively* engaged in organising a strike risk entailing extra-contractual liability. Whether trade unions merely calling for a strike can be considered as being actively engaged in organising a strike is a debated issue.[8]

Collective actions in general will give rise to massive economic damage to employers. Contrary to a widely held belief, however, they are not intended to cause damage. Collective actions intend to influence the behaviour and the policies of actors able to impact on the social and economic interests of workers. These actors include State as well as private actors.

The question arises to what extent collective actions tend to frustrate the establishment and functioning of (domestic) free market economies, let alone the sacrosanct Common Market. The *legal* relevance of such a question will depend upon the institutionalisation of the economic principles underpinning the establishment and the functioning of market economies. In domestic legal orders, the idea that the proper functioning of free markets calls for a prohibition of strikes takes us back to times immemorial.[9] The end of arts and crafts, which triggered the emergence of free capitalist market economies at the level of the Nation State, coincided with the penal prohibition of so-called conspiracies (*coalitions)* in order not to distort wage settings and prices as early as the adoption of the infamous *Loi Le Chapelier* (1791). The *délit de coalition* was integrated into the Napoleonic *Code Pénal*, which guaranteed that the penal prohibition became widespread throughout Europe. The *Code Pénal* assured the longevity of the criminal prohibition of collective action long after the termination of Napoleonic rule. In the second half of the nineteenth century, the *délit* was gradually abolished, however. The conceptual association between industrial actions and the distortion

6 P. Humblet, "Kort geding en collectief conflict. Diabolische procedure of laatste redmiddel tegen syndicaal hooliganisme?", in X, *De norm achter de regel* (Story-Scientia, Ghent, 1995), p. 154.

7 B. Palli, "French Labour law Report" in F. Dorssemont, T. Jaspers and A. Van Hoek, *Cross-Border Collective Actions in Europe: A Legal Challenge. A study on the legal aspects of transnational collective actions from a labour law and private international law perspective*, (Intersentia, Antwerp, 2007), p. 123.

8 In France, the liability of a trade union will be dependent upon effective participation in a wrongful strike, which presupposes that it has been actively involved in the organisation thereof. (Cass fr 9 November 1982 (*Dubigeon Normandie* and *Trailor*) [1983] *Droit social*, pp 175–177.

9 See A. Jacobs, "Collective Self-Regulation" in B. Hepple and P. O'Higgins, *The making of Labour Law in Europe,* (Mansell Publishing Limited, London and New York, 1986), pp. 196–207. Furthermore, see S. Webb and B. Webb, *The history of Trade Unionism* (Longmans, Green and Co, London, 1894) pp 57–161.

of economic order was abandoned. The perception of industrial action shifted from criminal to civil law. The penal prohibition of industrial action as an economic crime was only re-introduced due to perverted fascist regimes. But this experience was more short-lived than that of the *Code Pénal.*

Furthermore, the answer to the aforementioned question will depend on the question whether the ability to have recourse to social dumping is considered to be an essential prerequisite for the Freedom to Provide Services at the Common Market level or whether, on the contrary, combating social dumping is an essential element of the principles of Market Integration.[10] If the latter is the case, the fight against social dumping cannot restrict Market Integration. It will become an essential means to guarantee *fair* competition. A similar approach was adopted with regard to the Free Movement of Workers. The Free Movement of Workers is not considered to be restricted because migrant workers are not able to compete with the workers of the Host State through *Schmutzconcurrenz.* Their right to equal treatment is an essential means to safeguard the free Movement of Workers.[11]

The latter approach was not upheld by the Court. In *Laval* the Court explicitly restricted the notion of "fair competition" between service providers to the limited list contained in Article 3(1) of the Posting of Workers Directive.[12]

The approach is reminiscent of the approach adopted by Advocate General Maduro in his opinion in *Viking.* The Advocate General explicitly accepted the generic idea that the "realisation of economic progress through intra-Community trade involves the risk for workers [...] of having to undergo changes of working circumstances or even suffer the loss of their jobs".[13] In this respect a collective action in order to preclude social dumping was considered to be a restriction of Market Integration. The opinion deviates from Maduro's previous attempts to reconcile social rights with a proper functioning of the Common Market.[14] As far as Market Integration is concerned, social dumping appears to be of the essence. In *Viking*[15] the Court and Advocate General Mengozzi take a similar stance,

10 In the same vein, Bercusson formulates the quintessential question in both cases as follows: "Is the nature of the internal market envisaged by the Treaty such that the Collective Trade Union Action is to be regarded as a Restriction on, or as an integral and essential component of its effective functioning?". B. Bercusson (2006), pp. 290–294.

11 See Article 39 TEC and Article 7 EC Regulation no. 1612/68. See C. Barnard, *The substantive law of the EU,* (Oxford University Press, Oxford, 2004), pp. 274–276 and C. Barnard, EC *Employment Law,* (Oxford University Press, Oxford, 2006), pp. 195–197.

12 ECJ, C-341/05, 18 December 2007, (*Laval un Partneri Ltd v Svenska Byggnadsarbeterareförbundet and others*), §74. (Henceforth, referred to as the *Laval* judgment).

13 Opinion of Advocate General Maduro Case C-438/05.

14 M.P. Maduro, "Striking the Elusive Balance between Economic Freedom and Social Rights", in Ph. Alston, *The EU and Human Rights,* (Oxford University Press, Oxford, 1999) pp. 449–472.

15 ECJ, C-341/05, 18 December 2007, (*Laval un partneri Ltd v. Svenska Bggnadsarbeterförbundet and others*) (hereafter referred to as the *Viking* judgement).

insofar as the collective actions concerned *were* considered to constitute restrictions of Viking's freedom of establishment. Hence, both the Court and Advocate General Mengozzi agreed that the Freedom of Establishment does not seek to preclude social dumping. The Court and the Advocate General only disagreed about the extent to which combating social dumping can justify restrictions to the freedom to provide services. The fact that Mengozzi referred more frequently to the notion of "social dumping" is revealing in this respect.[16]

Collective actions are able to frustrate the functioning of free market economies in a *direct* as well as in an *indirect* way. Collective actions are a means to an end. The means as well as the end can obstruct fundamental freedoms. In general, recourse to collective action will not directly frustrate the functioning of free market economies. Insofar as the means of collective action amount to the blocking of public transport and roads, a *direct* threat to the free movement of goods is imminent. In general, collective actions intend to influence employers in two different ways. Collective actions can be undertaken in order to force an employer to conclude a collective agreement regulating working conditions on the labour market. The conclusion of collective agreements will restrict free competition between employees offering their services on the *labour* market. Other collective actions tend to influence the unilateral exercise of managerial prerogative. Restructuring and relocation constitute decisions which severely affect the interests of workers. Hence, collective actions can be undertaken to influence the behaviour of employers seeking to establish themselves in another Member State in order to provide services at the *Market of Services*. In both scenarios, an *indirect* impact on the functioning of markets emerges.

At first sight, the distinction between the Market of Services and the Labour Market might constitute an appealing criterion to demarcate legitimate and illegitimate collective actions. In such an approach, collective actions restricting competition on the Labour Market could be considered to be consistent with the so-called *Albany* immunity, whereas employers should be able to compete with one another without being hampered by collective action. In *Albany*[17], the Court granted an exemption from competition rules to the benefit of collective agreements regulating working conditions in line with the Social Policy objectives of the European Community.

In practice, the distinction between the Labour Market and the Market of Services is troublesome. In general, service providers will recruit workers in order to provide services. The situation will be different when they are self-employed service providers. The regulation of the working conditions applicable to those

16 See Opinion of Advocate General Mengozzi Case C-341/05, §4, 246, 249, 251, 273 280.

17 ECJ, C-67/99, 21 September 1999, (*Albany*).

workers will be an essential element in the decision of service providers to provide their services in a given Member State. Insofar as workers recruited in the State of origin will be posted by a transnational service provider in a Host State, the regulation of their working conditions by that Host State can render the exercise of their Freedom to Provide Services less attractive. In *Rush Portuguesa*[18], the Court indicated that workers who are temporarily posted fall outside the provisions relating to the Free Movement of Workers. Thus, the Court did not impose the Principle of Equal Treatment between posted workers and those workers who are permanently residing and working in the Host Country. *Rush Portuguesa* tends to grant immunity from the principle of Equal Treatment to the benefit of Service Providers based on the fallacy that the individual posted workers did not gain access to the Labour Market of the Host Country. The potential macro-impact that the posting of workers might have on the Labour Market of the Host Country was apparently ignored.

From a formal point of view, posted workers tend to be allocated to the Labour Market of their country of origin, while performing their work within the boundaries of another Member State effectively competing with workers of the Host Country on the basis of labour costs rather than on the basis of the productivity and the quality of their work.[19] Hence, the Court implicitly precluded *in nuce* a conflict between the Free Movement of Workers and the Freedom to Provide Services. Thus, the Court took a stance in favour of the Service Provider. Any salvation in order to uphold the Principle of Equal Treatment was bound to spring from the intervention of Member States[20] and/or trade unions. However, these interventions need to be in conformity with the freedom to provide services.[21] In the absence of any intervention, a situation of reverse discrimination to the disadvantage of native service providers of the Host State will emerge. The latter cannot invoke Free Movement principles in order to combat domestic labour standards or collective actions. Collective actions aimed at forcing the service provider to conclude an agreement or to accede to an existing agreement applicable in the Host State serve to combat social dumping which affects workers on the labour Market of the Host State.

---

18 ECJ, C-113/89, 27 March 1990, (*Rush Portuguesa*). See C.Barnard (2006), pp. 275–278.

19 ECJ, C-113/89, 27 March 1990, (*Rush Portuguesa*), §15.

20 See ECJ, C-113/89, 27 March 1990, (*Rush Portuguesa*) §18.

21 The requirement that these interventions are consistent with the freedom to provide services was upheld by the Court of Justice before as well as after the adoption and the implementation of the Posting of Workers Directive. On this issue: R. Giesen, "Posting: social protection of workers versus fundamental freedoms?", [2003], *CMLR* 143–158; M.S. Houwerzijl, *De detacheringsrichtlijn*, (Kluwer, Deventer, 2004), pp. 190–215; V. Hatzopoulos and T.U. Do, "The case law of the ECJ concerning the Free provision of services: 2000–2005", [2006], *CMLR* pp. 972–978. C. Barnard (2006), pp. 278–280.

3. THE RIGHT TO TAKE COLLECTIVE ACTION: FOUNDING FATHERS, JUDGES AND LEGISLATORS

Historically, the legal recognition of resorting to collective action in domestic legal orders has been a necessary prerequisite to prevent an action considered to be "at odds with the law" from being outlawed. From a technical point of view, two techniques can be used to avoid a clash with the principles of contract and tort law. A first technique consists of exempting employees from contractual liability and immunizing trade unions from liability under tort law. Thus the civil law techniques of contract and tort law *will not affect* any recourse to collective action. Employment protection against unfair dismissal and immunity for the benefit of trade unions need to be distinguished from recognising recourse to strike action or to collective action "in its own right". The latter, *id est* the recognition of a right to strike for the benefit of employees as well as the right of trade unions to organise a collective action will amount to the conclusion that neither contract law nor tort law *shall apply* to employees and trade unions resorting to collective action. The recourse to collective action will need to be considered as the exercise of a right, even more as the exercise of a *fundamental* workers' right. *Qui suo iure utitur, neminem laedit.*

In a recent comparative overview of the domestic recognition of the right to strike in nine Member States, the recourse to the first technique was shown to be restricted to the United Kingdom. Other Member States (Belgium, Finland, France, Germany, Italy, the Netherlands, Spain and Sweden) have opted for a clear-cut and more generous recognition of the right to strike, or of the right to take collective action as the case may be.[22] The difference between both techniques is often described by referring to the distinction between the *freedom* of collective action *vis-à-vis* the *right* to take collective action.[23] The *Monti* Regulation bears witness to that distinction deeply rooted in comparative labour law.[24] The legal recognition of collective action has recently been saluted as an intelligent means to ritualize the expression of social discontent. The recognition of some types of collective action offers a valid alternative to more violent expressions of social discontent.[25] Domestic legal orders have tried to privilege some *species* of collective

22 F. Dorssemont, "Labour law issues of transnational collective action – comparative report", in F. Dorssemont, T. Jaspers and A. Van Hoek (2007), pp. 252–254.

23 F. Dorssemont, (2007), pp. 245–254.

24 Article 2 of EC Regulation 2679/98 (Monti Regulation).

25 See in this respect, the phrase by Alain Supiot in his column in *Le Monde*, which provides the heading to this contribution. (A. Supiot, "Voilà l'économie communiste de marché", *Le Monde*, 25 January 2008).

actions considered to be "peaceful".[26] By their very nature omissions are more peaceful than actions which are in fact committed. In the same vein, the repression of an omission to act constitutes a more serious intrusion into personal freedom. Thus, the collective non-performance of the employment contract constitutes an omission to act. As such, it is an example of peaceful resistance. The circular at issue in *Viking* is another example of a peaceful action. ITF called upon its Members to refrain from concluding a collective agreement with the blacklisted shipowner.

At present, the domestic law governing collective action needs to be computed on the basis of a variety of legal sources. However, the *initial* legal recognition of the ability to have recourse to collective action in the Member States concerned was operated by distinct institutional actors. Such recognition was triggered either by the founding fathers, *id est* by Constitutional Assemblies, by Judges or, in a rare case (the United Kingdom), by the Legislator. It took place during distinct chronological eras due to different historical developments.

In France, Italy and Spain, constitutional recognition took place as an antithesis after fascist regimes had reintroduced criminal prohibitions on collective actions.

Judicial recognition took place in Germany, Belgium and the Netherlands. Statutory recognition through immunity and a restricted employment protection took place in the United Kingdom. The statutory immunity granted to trade unions took place by way of a *revanche sur la judiciaire.*

4. THE RIGHT TO TAKE COLLECTIVE ACTION IN EC LAW

4.1. EUROPE: TRANSCENDING OR IMPOSING LIMITS ON COLLECTIVE ACTION?

The question arises which institutional actors have taken a stance with regard to collective action at the level of the European Community, irrespective of whether or not such a stance has amounted to a formal recognition. In a powerful reflection regarding the legal challenges facing collective action from an EC Law perspective, Bercusson indicated how focusing on the different institutional actors can be

26 *Peaceful*: See International Labour Office Geneva, *Digest of decisions and principles of the Freedom of Association Committee of the Governing Body of the ILO, Freedom of Association*, Fifth (revised) edition, no. 545 See also R. Ben-Israel, *International Labour Standards*, (Kluwer Law and Taxation Publishers, Deventer, 1988), p. 117.

useful in understanding the present EU legal regime governing collective industrial action.[27] The relevance of EU Law for collective actions is twofold.

Divergencies between the domestic labour law of the Member States tend to complicate an effective recourse to *transnational* collective action in a European space. In this respect, the fact that the European Union lacks competence to adopt a minimum standard for the legality of a collective action complicates an effective recourse to transnational collective action. A legal pan-European strike would presuppose that trade unions and workers in all the Member States concerned will not be hampered by the state of their domestic law regulating collective action.[28] The question whether EU law can serve as a means to harmonise these divergencies in order to facilitate an effective recourse to collective action is relevant. In practice, these divergencies are already being exploited by those opposed to transnational collective action through the calculated use of the procedural (forum) and substantive (*applicable law*) aspects of Private International Law (PIL). Insofar as PIL allows for some flexibility in choosing a convenient forum or triggering the application of a convenient applicable law, the question arises whether *European Private International Law* can be used as a tool to reduce this kind of flexibility and to provide more legal security for the parties actively involved in industrial action. The recent regulation on the law applicable to non-contractual obligations (Rome II) provides a rare example of good practice. It has introduced a special PIL rule regarding non-contractual obligations in respect of the liability of a person in the capacity of a worker or an employer or the organisations representing their professional interests for damages caused by an industrial action which is either pending or has been carried out. The applicable law deviates from the generic *lex locus damni*.[29] Instead, Rome II has opted for the *lex locus actus*. The option will increase the ability of the actors engaged in collective action to foresee the legal outcome of a liability suit. There is a much greater probability that they will be familiar with the *lex locus actus* than with the *lex locus damni*. Collective action, not least transnational solidarity strikes, touches upon a network of contractual and non-contractual obligations. The fact that Rome I does not contain any specific PIL rule relating to contractual obligations which might spring from collective actions does not provide sufficient guarantees that the same law will govern the issue of the legitimacy of a collective action for all the actors involved irrespective of the nature of their legal relation

---

27 B. Bercusson, "Foreword. Restoring a Balance of Economic Power in Europe", in F. Dorssemont, T. Jaspers and A. Van Hoek, (2007), 5–8.

28 This observation has urged Giubonni and Orlandini to refute that subsidiarity could constitute a valid argument for upholding the exclusion of the right to strike enshrined in Article 137 5) TEC. See S. Giubboni and G. Orlandini, "Lo sciopero e l'Unione Europea. Appunti critici", [2005], *Lavori. Quaderni di Rassegna sindacale*, p. 294. In the same vein S. Giubboni (2006), 133–134.

29 In this respect: compare Article 4 and Article 9 of Regulation 864/2007 (Rome II).

with the plaintiff. The risk of party shopping in order to attack the weakest part of the chain in the network, *i.e.* the part of the chain governed by the most precarious applicable law, continues to be a very real one.[30]

In *Viking* and *Laval*, another dimension of the relevance of EC Law was paramount. Both employers invoked Free Movement principles in order to challenge collective actions undertaken in Sweden and Finland. These collective actions were perfectly consistent with applicable Swedish and Finnish Law. EC Law was considered by the employers to be an inspiring source for restrictions on collective actions which were unprecedented under domestic law. Hence, the issues at stake with regard to the recognition of collective action at EC Level are essentially different from those at the domestic level. Legal recognition at the EC level does *not* seek to shield collective actions from the principles of *domestic* contract and tort law. It seeks to shield collective actions to some extent from EC legal principles underpinning the process of Market Integration. As opposed to other European and international legal orders, the EU legal order has not generally been construed as a fountain of justice granting fundamental rights against the action of domestic States or even of other private actors. These European and international legal orders protect citizens against the actions of institutions located in domestic legal orders. The rationale behind a constitutional catalogue of human rights at the EC level is essentially different. It is similar to that of constitutional charters on the domestic level, protecting citizens against the institutions organised by that Constitution. Thus, the Charter of Nice's application is explicitly restricted to

> "the institutions, bodies, offices and agencies of the Union with due regard for the principle of subsidiarity and to the Member States only when they are implementing Union law. They shall therefore respect the rights, observe the principles and promote the application thereof in accordance with their respective powers and respecting the limits of the powers of the Union as conferred on it in the Treaties".[31]

At present, various institutions have taken a stance with regard to collective action. These various positions do not tackle all the issues raised above, however. Some of the positions regarding major issues are specific and to the point, whereas others have a more generic character. They might conflict with one another. These positions will be dealt with below.

---

30 For a joint contribution on the issue: See F. Dorssemont and A. Van Hoek, "De collectieve actie bij arbeidsconflicten in Rome II", [2008] *Revue de droit commercial,* forthcoming.

31 See Article 51(1) Charter of Fundamental Rights of the European Union.

4.2. PRIMARY EC LAW

From a chronological perspective, the oldest reference to the right to take collective action dates back to the Agreement on Social Policy (ASP) annexed to the Protocol on Social Policy. The latter is a constituent part of the Treaty of Maastricht (1992).[32] The provision was integrated into the body of the TEC by the amending the Treaty of Amsterdam (1997). The provision precludes the use of EC competences in the field of Social Policy (Title XI) to regulate "the right to strike" and "the right to impose lockouts." The generic competence which was explicitly recognised in the field of the collective defence of the interests of workers and employers could have warranted the conclusion that the European Community did have competence in this regard.

This reference obviously excludes any recourse to EC competences in the field of Social Policy to harmonise the divergences between the Member States in order to facilitate recourse to transnational strikes. The latter is astonishing insofar as the content of the ASP was based upon an agreement between the European Social Partners.[33] It is difficult to comprehend the motives behind the exclusion. It might have been inspired by a form of suspicion towards statutory intervention with regard to the exercise of the right to strike. Such an attitude is deeply rooted in anarchistic traditions. It becomes even more poignant in the field of a right which is considered to be at odds with the law. Another key issue for such an interpretation might be the idea that trade unions hoped that such an exclusion would shield existing systems of industrial relations from Community intervention. Such a hope does not seem to be warranted, however. The imminent threat to the domestic legal protection of the right to strike does not stem exclusively nor primarily from EC Directives which *directly* regulate the exercise of the right to strike. It stems from primary EC Law as well as from secondary EC Law regarding Free Movement. These provisions could produce a spillover effect restricting recourse to the right to strike.

A more appropriate way of shielding existing systems of industrial relations would have been to indicate in a constitutional provision that the EC Treaty could not be used to affect the right to strike and to engage in a lockout, insofar as the latter was recognised at Member State level. In a recent resolution, the Executive Committee of the ETUC has advocated the idea of integrating a so-called "social progress clause" into the TEC.[34] The idea had been propagated earlier on by the

32 C. Barnard, (2006), pp. 17–20 and J. Kenner, *EU Employment Law*, (Oxford and Portland, Oregon, 2003), pp. 223–226.

33 J. Kenner (2003), p. 246.

34 See www.etuc.org/IMG/pdf_ETUC_Viking_Laval_-_resolution_070308.pdf.
The following clause is proposed:

Secretary-General of the ETUC in a hearing at the Employment and Social Affairs Committee of the European Parliament.

For that reason, it is extremely difficult to refer to Article 137(5) in order to suggest that EC law could *not affect* or *does not apply* to collective action. Such an argument was indeed explicitly refuted by the Court of Justice in *Viking* and *Laval*.[35] The position of the Court is consistent with the extensive analysis devoted to this issue in the opinion of Advocate General Mengozzi.[36]

Article 137(5) TEC refers to two specific species of collective action. It does not *formally* exclude the EC's competence to intervene in order to regulate other types of collective action, such as contractual boycotts or physical blockades. The semantics of other language versions refers to the collective refusal to perform the employment contract (*cf.* "sciopero" (Italian), "grève" (French) and "staking" (Dutch)). From a formal perspective, exceptions need to be interpreted narrowly. Advocate General Mengozzi expressed his doubts as to whether the reservation in Article 137(5) TEC extends more generally to all collective actions.[37]

Authors have adopted divergent opinions with regard to the question whether Article 137(5) excludes any recourse to more generic and older provisions attributing competences to the EC.

Since the provision is a Lex specialis and a Lex posterior, it is difficult to assume that such recourse is compatible with the EC Treaty. In his opinion Mengozzi explicitly argued that Article 137(5) TEC precludes any recourse to general provisions of the EC Treaty to regulate the right to strike.[38]

"Nothing in the Treaty, and in particular neither fundamental freedoms nor competition rules shall have priority over fundamental social rights and social progress. In case of conflict, fundamental social rights shall take precedence.
Economic freedoms cannot be interpreted as granting undertakings the right to exercise them for the purpose or with the effect of evading or circumventing national social and employment laws and practices or for social dumping.
Economic freedoms, as established in the Treaties, shall be interpreted in such a way as not infringing upon the exercise of fundamental social rights as recognised in the Member States and by Community/Union law, including the right to negotiate, conclude and enforce collective agreements and to take collective action, and as not infringing upon the autonomy of social partners when exercising these fundamental rights in pursuit of social interests and the protection of workers."

35 *Viking* judgement, §41 and *Laval* judgement §88.

36 Opinion of AG Mengozzi, §57.

37 Opinion of AG Mengozzi §57.

38 Opinion of AG Mengozzi §57: "If the effectiveness of Article 137 5) EC is to be upheld, the Community institutions could not of course resort to other legal bases in the Treaty in order to adopt measures designed to approximate the laws of the Member States in this field". In the same vein: J. Kenner, (2003), 533; T. Novitz, *International and European Protection of the right to strike*, (Oxford University Press, Oxford, 2003), p. 162. *Contra:* Roger Blanpain, *European Labour Law*, (Kluwer Law International, The Hague, 2000) p. 26. On this issue, see also the Ph.

In sum, the reference to the right to strike and the right to engage in a lockout in the context of a description of EC competences can hardly be used as a conclusive argument for recognising the right to strike as a fundamental right, hence a general principle of EC law recognised at the EC level. The recognition of the right to take collective action in the Nice Charter on Fundamental Rights of the European Union[39] *does* constitute a compelling reason to construe such a recognition. The amending Treaty of Lisbon has corroborated this argument, stating that "The Union recognises the rights, freedoms and principles set out in the Charter of Fundamental Rights of the European Union of 7 December 2000, as adapted at Strasbourg, on 12 December 2007, which shall have the same legal value as the Treaties".[40]

A future compelling reason to assume that the right to take collective action needs to be construed as a fundamental right at the EC level is the accession of the European Union to the European Convention on Human Rights. The Lisbon Treaty imposes a constitutional duty on the European Union to accede to the European Convention on Human Rights.

It is still unclear whether such an accession will urge the Court of Justice to reassess the momentum attached to fundamental rights in its ruling on cases regarding conflicting EC legal principles. Insofar as some of these general principles are rooted in the ECHR, the question will arise whether they can merely be "balanced" against economic fundamental freedoms. Member States which have acceded to the ECHR hold different views on the question whether the ECHR has primacy *vis-à-vis* the constitutional and even the statutory rules of their legal order. Nevertheless, in the near future the following question will inevitably arise: to what extent will the Strasbourg European Court of Human Rights consider such a balancing act to be compatible with the ECHR? In the meantime, trade unions might take the opportunity to challenge the assessments of the Court of Justice in a more indirect way on the basis of the final judgements of the referring judges in *Laval* and *Viking* in a procedure against Sweden and the United Kingdom instigated before the Strasbourg Court. It might be an interesting prospect to address the issue before the European Committee on Social Rights first.

The right to take collective action has not been explicitly enshrined within the ECHR. The question arises to what extent the right to take collective action is covered and protected by the recognition in Article 11 ECHR of the "freedom of

D thesis by J. Hellsten, "From Internal Market Regulation to *ordre communautaire social*" in J. Hellsten From Internal Market Regulation to European Labour Law, 91–98. https://oa.doria.fi/bitstream/handle/10024/29178/frominte.pdf?sequence=1.

39 Charter of Fundamental Rights of the European Union, Official Journal C 303 of 14 December 2007.

40 See Article 6 consolidated version of the Treaty on European Union.

association including the right to form and to join trade unions for the protection of his interests".[41] For decades, this question boiled down to the assessment whether the right to strike was either just an important or rather an essential means to protect workers' interests. Insofar as it was just considered to be an important means, the ECHR was satisfied to detect the existence of other means to protect workers' interests. If these means existed, restrictions on the right to strike were not scrutinized by the Court.[42] In the *Unison* decision, the Court took a different stance. Without altering its assessment that the right to strike constituted just an important means to protect workers' interests, it did decide to make these restrictions subject to the scrutiny under Article 11 §2 ECHR.[43] As Ewing rightly pointed out, such an approach constitutes progress.[44] It means that the right to strike *does* fall within the scope of Article 11 ECHR. This approach was corroborated in the more authoritative *Dilek* judgement. Furthermore, on that occasion the Court took the step to extend the protection granted to the right to strike to the more generic right to take collective action. The Court avoided a doctrinal debate as to whether the collective action concerned did in fact constitute a strike. Such an academic discourse is not relevant insofar as the collective action (*id est* a refusal by civil servants to fulfil their *service de péage*) could be considered to be covered by the right to take collective action. In practice, this approach amounts to the conclusion that restrictions on the right to collective action need to be compatible with Article 11 §2 ECHR.[45]

However, the formal recognition of the right to take collective action as a *general principle* of EC Law does not shed sufficient light on the relation between such a general principle and conflicting fundamental economic freedoms.

4.3. SECONDARY EC LAW

In the second half of the 1990s the European "legislator" took a formal stance regarding the relationship between the right to take collective action and some Free Movement principles enshrined in the Posting of Workers Directive 96/71 (PWD) and the *Monti* Regulation 2679/98. In the 22nd recital of the PWD, the

---

41 See F. Dorssemont, "De vakverenigingsvrijheid ex artikel 11 EVRM, méér dan een sequel van de vrijheid van vereniging?", *Arbeidsrechtelijke annotaties*, [2006/2], pp. 25–31 and J.P. Marguénaud and J. Mouly, "Les incursions de la Cour européenne des droits de l'homme en droit du travail : une œuvre encore en demi-teinte", [2008], *Revue de Droit du Travail* 19–21.

42 ECHR, 6 February 1976, *Schmidt en Dahlström v. Sweden* and ECHR 6 February 1976, *Swedish Engine Drivers' Union v. Sweden*.

43 ECHR, 10 January 2002, *Unison v United Kingdom*, no. 53574/99.

44 K. Ewing, "The implication of Wilson and Palmer" [2003], *Industrial Law Journal*, p. 18.

45 ECHR, 17 July 2007, *Dilek and others v. Turkey* nos. 74611/01, 26876/06 and 27628/02 (the case was previously published under the name *Satilmis*).

legislator explicitly stated that the Directive is "without prejudice to the law of the Member States concerning collective action to defend the interests of trades and professions". In the *Monti* Regulation, a similar clause was formally integrated into the binding provisions of the Regulation.[46]

The philosophy of these instruments is unambiguous. Neither the PWD related to the Freedom to Provide Services nor the *Monti* Regulation can be used *to affect* the level of protection granted to collective actions by domestic law. These provisions do *not* recognise collective action as a *general principle* of *EC Law*. They do provide immunity to domestic law from instruments related to Free Movement. The provisions do *not* state that the instruments *will not apply*. If they would not apply, no clause providing immunity would have been needed. Thus, the legislator gives the impression of broadening the scope of the exclusion laid down in Article 137(5) applicable to EC competences in the field of Social Competences. It acted as if other Treaty provisions conferring competences also do not allow the legislator to impede the domestic recognition of the right to take collective action.[47] A spillover effect is thus being prevented. This attitude provides proof of prudent abstentionism. From an institutional point of view, this reluctance is consistent with the Community legislator's constitutional inability to intervene in a direct way[48] with regard to the right to strike.

In *Laval* both Advocate General Mengozzi as well as the Court of Justice completely ignored the existence of the 22nd recital of the PWD. The Court's approach is puzzling since it took the recitals of the PWD into account, albeit in a selective way. Instead, the Court argued that collective actions had to be held to be incompatible with the isolated provisions of the PWD.[49] A clause providing for immunity laid down in a Directive or Regulation will not be sufficient to guarantee

46 Article 2 of that Regulation unambiguously states:
"This Regulation may not be interpreted as affecting in any way the exercise of fundamental rights as recognised in Member States, including the right or freedom to strike. These rights may also include the right or freedom to take other actions covered by the specific industrial relations systems in Member States".

47 For the PWD: the articles which formed the basis of its adoption are Articles 55 and 47 TEC (the current article numbers). For the *Monti* Regulation, the legal basis was Article 308 TEC (the current article number).

48 In this perspective, the European Union could be seen as having competence to legislate on strike action in a more indirect way, *id est* regarding issues which do not directly affect the legitimacy of the *right to strike*. The aforementioned Article 9 of Rome II provides evidence of such an understanding. The Article is only relevant for the issue of conflict rules. Hence, recital 28 of the Regulation provides: (28) The special rule on industrial action in Article 9 is without prejudice to the conditions relating to the exercise of such action in accordance with national law and without prejudice to the legal status of trade unions or of the representative organisations of workers as provided for in the law of the Member States.

49 *Laval* judgment, §121.

that collective action will be exempted from Free Movement principles enshrined in the TEC.[50] This consideration might explain why the Court was not impressed by the *formula* providing for immunity. It warrants a constitutional immunity clause as propagated by the ETUC.

In the recent Services Directives 2006/123 the legislator opted for a more cautious *formula* which respects, in a redundant way, the primacy of the TEC above secondary EC instruments. Article 2(7) states that the Services Directive "does not affect the right to negotiate, conclude and enforce collective agreements and to take industrial action in accordance with national law and practices *which respect Community law*". However, the *formula* is preceded by a more generic clause which states that the Directive "does not affect the exercise of fundamental rights as recognised in the Member States and by Community law."

The semantic difference is puzzling for two obvious reasons. It gives the impression that the right to take collective action is a contrario not a fundamental right recognised in the Member States and by Community Law. Furthermore, it seems to suggest that fundamental rights are recognised in their own right, even if they do *not* respect Community Law. In the fourteenth recital of the Services Directive, the issue of "industrial action" is downgraded as an issue of ordinary labour standards under the *rubrica* of industrial relations and it is repeated that it is part of the enumerative definition of labour law in Article 2(6).

The juxtaposition in the Services Directive of the *formula* "does not affect" opposite the formula "shall not apply"[51] confirms our scholastic approach to the distinction between an immunity and an exclusion from the sphere of application.

4.4. THE COURT OF JUSTICE

Despite the fact that judges have historically been major institutional actors in recognising the right to strike, the Court of Justice has cautiously avoided doing so.[52] The recent judgements in *Laval* and *Viking* constitute a symbolic landmark.

---

50 In this respect, see the intelligent observations by J. Hellsten, "On the social dimension in Posting of Workers" 72–73 in J. Hellsten, From Internal Market Regulation to European Labour Law. https://oa.doria.fi/bitstream/handle/10024/29178/frominte.pdf?sequence=1.
The author explicitly states: "Hence, whereas no secondary EC legislation can overrule the Treaty, the logical conclusion in this broader context is that recital 22 of the PWD does not guarantee any full immunity for national rules on strikes or industrial actions in general".

51 Compare Articles 1 and 2 of the Services Directive.

52 See T. Novitz, *International and European Protection of the right to strike* (Oxford University Press, Oxford, 2003) pp. 245–260. Also E. Franssen, *Legal Aspects of the European Social Dialogue*, (Intersentia, Antwerp, 2002), pp 8–10.

In both judgements, the Court construed the right to take collective action on behalf of workers as a general principle of EC Law.[53]

The aforementioned judicial *pudeur* is omnipresent in other famous cases where the issue of fundamental workers' rights lay at the heart of the debate. The Court has never specifically recognised the freedom of a *trade union* association. In *Bosman*, the Court recognised the freedom of association in a generic way.[54] In *Werhof*, it recognised the *negative* freedom of association for the benefit of employers.[55] In *Werhof* that negative freedom of collective bargaining was approached as a *correlarium* to the freedom of association. The Court based that assessment by referring to the ECHR *Gustaffson* case.[56] A proper reading of the *Gustaffson* case shows that compelling an employer to conclude a tie-in agreement does *not* constitute a violation of the freedom of association. Mengozzi's reading of the *Gustaffson* case is much more accurate in this regard.[57] The reference to *Gustaffson* as an argument to outlaw boycott actions such as those at issue in *Laval* (intended to force an employer to conclude a tie-in agreement) is erroneous.[58] In his opinion in *Albany*, however, the Advocate General did construe *trade union freedom* as a general principle of EC law.[59] In previous staff cases, the Court had recognised the freedom of trade union association as a general principle of labour law. Such recognition is not equivalent to recognition as a general principle of EC law, however.[60]

The record of the Court in recognising the freedom of collective bargaining as a general principle is also poor. Although the approach of the Court in *Albany*[61] has, to a large extent, shielded the freedom of collective bargaining from intrusion by Competition principles, the Court did not take that occasion to state that the freedom of collective bargaining was a general principle which needed to be taken

---

53 See *infra* 6.5.

54 See ECJ, C-415/93, 15 October 1995 (*Bosman*), §79.

55 See ECJ, C-499/04, 9 March 2006, (*Werhof*) §33. For a comment on *Werhof* regarding the negative freedom of association: F. Dorssemont, "De vakverenigingsvrijheid ex artikel 11 EVRM, méér dan een sequel van de vrijheid van vereniging?", [2006], 2, *Arbeidsrechtelijke annotaties*, pp. 16–17. For a comprehensive comment on the judgment: R.M. Beltzer, "Overgang van cao-bepalingen: bevriezing of dynamiek", [2006], 2, *Arbeidsrechtelijke annotaties*, pp. 52–62.

56 ECHR, 25 April 1996, *Gustafsson versus Sweden*, no. 15573/89.

57 See the Opinion of Advocate General Mengozzi (*Laval*), §§275–2777.

58 N. Reich's reference in this regard to *Gustaffson* as an argument to outlaw the boycott action at issue in *Laval* is not entirely convincing. N. REICH (2008), pp. 129–131.

59 See the Opinion of AG Jacobs, 28 January 1999 (*Albany*, C-67/96; *Brentjes*, C-115/97 tot C-117/97, *Drijvende Bokken*, C-219/97), §158.

60 See ECJ, C-175/73, 8 October 1974, (*Union Syndicale*); ECJ, C-193/87 and C-194/87, 18 January 1990, (*Maurissen and Union Syndicale*). Article 24(a) of the Staff Regulations does recognise the freedom of association for the benefit of EC staff members.

61 ECJ, C-67/96, 21 September 1999 (*Albany*). (Hereafter referred to as the *Albany* judgement).

into account. In fact, the construction of a so-called "immunity"[62] did not necessitate that the Court should assess the issue whether the freedom of collective bargaining did constitute a general principle. In *Albany*, there was no need at all to make such a statement, since a clash between competition rules and the freedom of collective bargaining was formally avoided.

In his opinion in *Albany*, the Advocate General refuted the idea that the freedom of collective bargaining could be protected in a specific manner. He argued that "it cannot be said that there is sufficient convergence of national legal orders and international legal instruments on the recognition of a specific fundamental right to bargain collectively".[63] Furthermore, he stated that the necessity to construe such a recognition was obsolete, since "the collective bargaining process, like any other negotiation between economic actors, is [...] sufficiently protected by the general principle of freedom of contract." In a way which prefigures *Schmidberger*, the AG stated that "the mere recognition of a fundamental right to bargain collectively would therefore not suffice to shelter collective bargaining from the applicability of the competition rules". He argued that the freedom of collective bargaining was sufficiently protected as an expression of the generic freedom to contract.[64] Such an approach to the collective agreement is at odds with the very quintessence of collective bargaining. It disregards the fact that collective agreements need to be seen as the exercise of collective autonomy granted to trade unions in their own right. In concluding collective agreements, these actors do not operate as agents of the affiliated workers. Furthermore, Jacobs' opinion blurs the distinction between general principles. Some general principles raise a human rights issue. It is far from obvious that the freedom to contract raises such an issue at all.

In UEAPME the Court recognised an essential aspect of the freedom of collective bargaining, *id est* the voluntary character of mutual recognition.[65] In UEAPME, the Court of first instance thus took a stance which was favourable to the principle of free and voluntary collective bargaining. It did not dispute that social partners have the freedom *not* to engage in a bargaining process with one another. The Court did not use the occasion to recognise the freedom of collective bargaining as a general principle of EC Law. It rather omitted to pay any attention to the underlying principle of the freedom of collective autonomy.

---

62 AG Maduro refers to the *Albany* ruling in terms of an "anti-trust immunity". In our view, immunity presupposes that the free competition rules are applicable. The Court in *Albany* rejected that *thesis*. See §27 Opinion of AG Maduro in *Viking*.

63 See §160 Opinion of AG Jacobs in *Albany*.

64 See §§160–161 Opinion of AG Jacobs in *Albany*.

65 Court of First Instance, 17 June 1998, no. T-135/96, Jur. II-2335 (UEAPME).

5. THE RIGHT TO TAKE COLLECTIVE ACTION *V.* FUNDAMENTAL FREEDOMS. FROM *SPANISH STRAWBERRIES* TO THE PRELIMINARY REFERENCES IN *LAVAL* AND *VIKING*

5.1. *SPANISH STRAWBERRIES* AND *SCHMIDBERGER*

The recognition of the right to take collective action as a general principle of EC Labour Law does not clarify whether an alleged clash between that right and the fundamental economic freedoms underlying the Common Market is conceivable and how this alleged conflict needs to be legally construed. The idea that the right to take collective action could clash with the Free Movement of Goods was made explicit in the *Monti* Regulation. Article 2 contains a clause which provides immunity to the right and or freedom of collective action recognised in Member States. Such immunity presupposes a conflict between the Free Movement of Goods which the Regulation seeks to safeguard and the right to take collective action.

The *Monti* Regulation[66] was adopted in the aftermath of the judgement in *Spanish Strawberries*.[67] The case concerned an infraction procedure initiated by the Commission against the Republic of France. The Commission expressed its discontent concerning "the passivity of the French authorities in face of violent acts committed by private individuals and by protest movements of French farmers directed against agricultural products from other Member States. Those acts consisted, inter alia, in the interception of lorries transporting such products in France and the destruction of their loads, violence against lorry drivers, threats against French supermarkets selling agricultural products originating in other

66 See: F. Schnorkop, "Neuer Interventionsmechanismus der Kommission zur Gewährleistung der Warenverkehrsfreiheit", [1998], *EuZW*, 237–242; G. Orlandini, "The Free Movement of Goods as a Possible Community limitation on industrial Conflict", [2000] *European Law Journal*, 352–361.
See the report by the European Commission regarding the application of COM (2001) 160 final. The report is analysed in: C. Gimeno Verdejo "La réponse communautaire aux blocages des résaux de transport : application et perspectives d'avebir du règlement n° 2679/98 en vue de la protection du marché intérieur", [2002], *Cahiers de droit européen*, 45–93.

67 ECJ, 9 December 1997, C 265/95, Commission *versus* Republic of France.
For a comment: B.J. Drijber, "Hof houdt lidstaat aansprakelijk voor niet-optreden tegen acties van particulieren", [1998] *Nederlands Tijdschrift voor Europees recht* 101–103; M. A. Jarvis, annotation [1998], *Common Market Law Review* 1371–1383; K.J.M. Mortelmans, "Artikel 5 EG juncto artikel 30 EG: een nieuwe route voor het vrije verkeer van goederen", [1998] *Ars Aequi* K. Muylle "Angry Farmers and Passive Policemen; Private Conduct and the Free Movement of Goods", [1998] *European Law Review*, 467–474; G. Orlandini, (2000), 341–352; J. Schwarze, "Zum Anspruch der Gemeinschaft auf polizeiliches Einschreiten der Mitgliedstaaten bei Störungen des grenzüberschreitenden Warenverkehrs durch Private", [1998] Europarecht 53–59.

Member States, and the damaging of those goods when on display in shops in France".[68]

The Court made it abundantly clear that the Free Movement of Goods does not only entail an obligation for Member States to refrain from interventions restricting the Free Movement, but that it also obliges a State to ensure the freedom of intra-Community trade in agricultural products on its territory by preventing and effectively dissuading the perpetrators of the offences in question from committing and repeating them.[69] In other words, an omission to react against a "collective action" by French farmers could amount to State liability as well.

This interpretation of the obligations flowing from the Treaty Provisions on Free Movement was codified in the *Monti* Regulation.[70] Furthermore, the Regulation introduces a monitoring procedure involving the Member States and the Commission with regard to obstacles to the Free Movement of Goods.

In casu, the "collective action" which had been strived at for over a decade could not have been covered by the constitutional and/or international recognition of the right to take collective action for two obvious reasons.

First, the right to take collective action is attributed to workers and/or employers. The French farmers were not acting in such a capacity. Secondly, the nature of their guerrilla actions was too violent to warrant the conclusion that the actions could be covered by Article 6 §4 European Social Charter.

The idea that a "collective action" obstructing the free movement of goods could raise a human rights issue became apparent in another *cause célèbre.* In *Schmidberger*[71], a German transport company started a liability suit against the

68 ECJ, 9 December 1997, C 265/95, Commission *versus* Republic of France, §2.

69 ECJ, 9 December 1997, C 265/95, Commission *versus* Republic of France, §32.

70 Article 4 Monti Regulation.

71 ECJ, C-112/2000, 12 June 2003 (Eugen Schmidberger versus Republik Osterreich). See the following Comments: A. Alemanno, annotation [2003] 2, *Revue du droit de l'Union européenne* 523–527, C. Brown, annotation, [2003], *Common Market Law Review* 1499–1510; F Dorssemont, "Met de vlam in de pijp. Vrijheid van vergadering en meningsuiting, recht op collectieve actie versus vrij verkeer/primaat of belangenafweging?", [2004], 1, *Arbeidsrechtelijke annotaties,* 77–94, B.J. Drijber, "Botsende vrijheden op de Brenner", [2003], *Nederlands tijdschrift voor Europees Recht,* 229–232; B. Koch, annotation [2003], *Europäische Zeitschrift für Wirtschaftsrecht,* 598–599; S. Kadelbach and N. Petersen, "Europäische Grundrechte als Schranken der Grundfreiheiten", [2003], *Europäische Grundrechte-Zeitschrift,* 693–698; F. Kessler, annotation [2003], *Revue de Jurisprudence sociale,* 751–754; K.J.M. Mortelmans, "De Brenner Pas: het vrije verkeer, het leefmilieu en de vrijheid van meningsuiting", [2003] *Ars Aequi,* 882–890; A. Woltjer, annotation [2003] 8, *European Human Rights Cases,* 595–597 and T. Georgopoulos, [2004] 6, *Petites affiches. La Loi/Le Quotidien juridique,* 11–14. Furthermore: J. Morijn, "Balancing Fundamental Rights and Common Market Freedoms in Union Law:

Austrian Government. The company objected to the passive stance adopted by the Austrian Government with regard to a "collective action" undertaken by an ecological action group called *Transitforum Austria Tirol* when it blocked access to the Brenner Motorway for 30 hours. The ecological group wanted to protest against the pollution which transport generated. According to the plaintiff, the Austrian Government was supposed to prevent such an obstruction of the Free Movement of Goods. Instead, the Government of Austria decided to authorise the "demonstration" which had been duly notified.

The Court decided that the demonstration in question did raise a human right issue. Despite the fact that the preliminary questions did not *explicitly* articulate the existence of such a clash, the Court rephrased these questions within the framework of a conflict between fundamental freedoms and human rights. It considered that the Austrian Government was "inspired" by its wish to respect fundamental rights, *id est* the freedom of expression[72] and the freedom of assembly. Both freedoms were recognised as general principles of EC Law which might justify, in principle, a restriction to the free movement of goods.[73]

Instead of establishing a clear-cut hierarchy between the Free Movement of Goods and the fundamental rights concerned, the Court decided to assess whether "a fair balance" had been struck by the Austrian Government.[74] It sought to opt for an avenue to reconcile conflicting requirements stemming from the Free Movement of Goods and those arising from the necessity to safeguard fundamental rights.

The key to such an assessment is a proportionality test. In *Schmidberger*, the Court *effectively* applied the proportionality test to the facts of the case at hand. Thus, the test was not merely prescribed for the benefit of the referring judge. The Court examined whether the restrictions on the free movement of goods could be justified by a pressing social need and were in particular *proportionate* to the legitimate aim pursued.[75] The necessity to safeguard the freedom of expression and assembly was considered to constitute a legitimate aim. The Court explicitly stated that the specific aim of the demonstration, *id est* the protection of the biosphere, was in itself immaterial in legal proceedings such as those instituted by

Schmidberger and Omega in the Light of the European Constitution", [2006], *European Law Journal*, 15–40.

72 ECJ, C-112/2000, 12 June 2003 (*Eugen Schmidberger versus Republik Osterreich*) §69. The reference to the freedom of expression is entirely absent in the preliminary questions.

73 ECJ, C-112/2000, 12 June 2003 (*Eugen Schmidberger versus Republik Osterreich*), §74.

74 ECJ, C-112/2000, 12 June 2003 (*Eugen Schmidberger versus Republik Osterreich*), §§77 and 81.

75 ECJ, C-112/2000, 12 June 2003 (*Eugen Schmidberger versus Republik Osterreich*), §82.

Schmidberger.[76] Hence, the Court did not take a teleological approach to proportionality. It did not examine for what purposes *Transit Forum* had decided to rely on their freedom of expression and the freedom of assembly. Nevertheless, the Court took into consideration that the "purpose of that public demonstration was not to restrict trade in goods of a particular type or from a particular source".[77]

In assessing the proportionality of the demonstration, the Court took a procedural as well as a substantive approach to proportionality.[78] The description of the relevant features of the demonstration tends to mirror the facts in Spanish Strawberries in a negative way. From a procedural point of view, the Court and the Advocate General considered that the demonstration had been *notified* to the public by means of an extensive publicity campaign. Thus, the economic operators concerned were duly informed of the traffic restrictions applying on the date and at the site of the proposed demonstration and were in a position to take all the necessary steps to circumvent those restrictions. In the same vein, the Court considered the fact that various administrative and supportive measures had been taken by the competent authorities in order to limit, as far as possible, the disruption to road traffic.

The Advocate General and the Court applied, although less explicitly, an *ultimum remedium* test. They considered that *Transit forum* did not have an alternative means to express its views in an equally effective manner.[79] They considered that there was no means for the demonstrators to make their point known which would have obstructed the free movement of goods in a less drastic way, without depriving the action of a substantial part of its impact.

The proportionality test also implies a more substantial assessment of the merits of the case. The Court considered the extent of the damage to the free movement of goods. The latter was limited by a comparison with both the geographic scale and the intrinsic seriousness of the disruption caused in the case of *Commission* v *France*.[80] Thus, the demonstration did not give rise to a general climate of insecurity so as to have a dissuasive effect on intra-Community trade flows as a whole, in contrast to the serious and repeated disruptions to public order at issue

---

76 ECJ, C-112/2000, 12 June 2003 (*Eugen Schmidberger versus Republik Osterreich*), Compare §66 and 86. See also the Opinion of the Advocate General Jacobs in *Schmidberger* §54 and §80, 81.

77 ECJ, C-112/2000, 12 June 2003 (*Eugen Schmidberger versus Republik Osterreich*), §86.

78 ECJ, C-112/2000, 12 June 2003 (Eugen Schmidberger versus Republik Osterreich), §§84–88.

79 See §110 and 118 of the Conclusion of Advocate General Jacobs in *Schmidberger* and ECJ, C-112/2000, 12 June 2003 (*Eugen Schmidberger versus Republik Osterreich*) §§89, 90 and 92.

80 ECJ, C-112/2000, 12 June 2003 (*Eugen Schmidberger versus Republik Osterreich*), §§83, 84 and 85.

in *Commission* v *France*. The economic damage suffered by Schmidberger was not taken into account as such.

5.2. PRELIMINARY REFERENCES IN *LAVAL* AND *VIKING*

5.2.1. A Comparison

In September and December 2007 the Swedish *Arbetsdomstolen* and the London Court of Appeal referred a preliminary reference to the Court of Justice. Both cases concern collective actions conflicting with basic Free Movement principles. In this respect, they are reminiscent of *Spanish Strawberries* and *Schmidberger*. However, they need to be distinguished according to two points of view. The collective actions which lie at the heart of *Laval* and *Viking* had been organised by trade unions. As opposed to farmers and ecological groups, employees were at the forefront. Hence, the human rights issues concerned immediately affect the right to take collective action which is restricted to employees, employers and their organisations. Whereas the Free Movement of Goods lay at the heart in *Spanish Strawberries* and *Schmidberger*, the Freedom to Provide Services was at stake in *Laval*. In *Viking* a shipowner invoked his Freedom of Establishment as a prerequisite to provide services.[81] Last but not least, the constellation of the parties is significantly different. In *Spanish Strawberries* and *Schmidberger*, a State's liability was under attack from the Commission and from a Transport Company for not having dealt with private organisations obstructing the free movement of goods. In *Laval* and *Viking* private employers invoked Free Movement provisions directly against trade unions. Hence, the issue of the horizontal effect of Free Movement provisions is at stake.

5.2.2. Viking

Viking, a company incorporated under Finnish law, operated seven vessels, including the *Rosella*. This vessel, sailing under a Finnish flag, sailed between Tallinn (Estonia) and Helsinki (Finland). The crew of the vessel were covered by a collective agreement which had been concluded with the Finnish trade union FSU. The company intended to reflag the *Rosella* by registering the vessel in either Estonia or Norway, in order to be able to enter into a new collective agreement with a trade union established in one of those States. Viking's plans were notified

81 In the preliminary questions of *Viking*, the Court was asked to assess the boycott action in the light of provisions related to the freedom of establishment as well as in the light of those related to the freedom to provide services. The Court indicated that the issues related to the freedom to provide services were premature, since in this case they could only become relevant after the reflagging had taken effect. *Viking* judgement, §30–31.

to the FSU and to the crew of the *Rosella*. The crew feared that the operation might entail collective redundancies. Furthermore, the Viking's plans were at odds with the Flag of Convenience Campaign[82] of the International Transport Workers' Federation. The ITF is suspicious of flags which do not correspond to the State where the beneficial ownership and the control over the vessel are situated. Such a flag is considered to be a flag of convenience. In accordance with ITF policy, only unions established in the State of the beneficial ownership have the right to conclude collective agreements covering the vessel concerned. In this particular scenario of a reflagging to another State, the ITF issued a circular to its affiliates not to conclude a collective agreement with the blacklisted subsidiary of the beneficial owner. The "collective action" of the affiliates called for by the ITF boils down to a co-ordinated exercise of the freedom *not* to engage in a process of collective bargaining.

Fearing that the reflagging operation might entail collective redundancies, FSU gave notice that it intended to organise a strike in order to secure jobs on the Rosella and in order to enforce the conclusion of a new collective agreement. Indeed, it considered that the applicable collective agreement had ended. As a result of the subsequent mediation procedure, Viking put an end to the dispute on 2 December 2003 by accepting the trade union's demands. The reflagging of the *Rosella* was suspended. FSU decided to withdraw the call to strike. No strike therefore took place. In line with the FOC campaign, the ITF refused to withdraw the circular.

Since the *Rosella* continued to run at a loss, Viking pursued its intention to reflag the vessel to Estonia. Because the ITF circular remained in force, on account of the fact that the ITF had never withdrawn it, the request to affiliated unions from the ITF in relation to the *Rosella* consequently remained in effect.

On 18 August 2004, Viking brought an action before the High Court of Justice of England and Wales, in the Queen's Bench Division (Commercial Court) requesting it to declare that the action taken by ITF and FSU was contrary to Article 43 EC, to order the withdrawal of the ITF circular and to order FSU not to infringe the rights which Viking enjoys under Community law. The competence of the British judicature flows from the fact that the defendant ITF was incorporated in the UK. By its decision of 16 June 2005, that court granted the order sought by Viking on the ground that the actual and threatened collective action by the ITF and FSU imposed restrictions on the freedom of establishment contrary to Article 43 EC and, in the alternative, constituted unlawful restrictions on the

82 See P. Chaumette (2008), 218–219 and D. Fitzpatrick, "Transnational collective action: the FOC Campaign, case study", in F. Dorssemont, T. Jaspers and A. Van Hoek (Intersentia, Antwerp, 2007), 85–92. Furthermore, see: www.itfglobal.org/flags-convenience/index.cfm.

freedom of movement for workers and the freedom to provide services under Articles 39 and 49 EC.

On 30 June 2005, ITF and FSU lodged an appeal against that decision before the referring court.

5.2.3. *Laval*

In *Laval*, a Latvian company had successfully established a subsidiary in Sweden.

The subsidiary, L & P Baltic Bygg, was awarded a public works contract following a tendering procedure for the renovation and the extension of school premises in the town of Vaxholm. The construction work was carried out by workers posted from Latvia to work on Swedish soil. The contract between Vaxholm and the Latvian subsidiary explicitly provided that Swedish collective agreements and tie-in agreements were applicable to the workers working on the building site. In practice, that clause was not respected by the Latvian company. Instead, it decided to apply a Latvian collective agreement with a Latvian trade union to the posted workers concerned. The collective agreement was concluded *after* the start of the building work.

The Swedish trade union representing the construction sector expressed its discontent concerning the fact that Baltic Bygg had refused to apply the conditions of its collective agreements. It invited Baltic Bygg to conclude a tie-in agreement (*hängavtal*). The company refused to do so. As a result, the posted workers were not covered by any Swedish instrument relating to minimum wages. There was no statutory legislation setting minimum wages. Furthermore, according to the Swedish system of collective bargaining, there was no means to declare a sectoral collective agreement generally binding. In fact, wage negotiations take place at the level of the undertaking, with the exception of a fall-back clause in the sectoral collective agreement. Baltyc Bygg was not a party to such an agreement.

As a result, the Swedish trade union representing the building sector gave notice of a boycott of all construction work at all Laval construction sites. Furthermore, the Swedish electricians' union joined the boycott in order to express its solidarity. The boycott amounted to a refusal by Swedish workers to perform their contract of employment for the benefit of Baltic Bygg as a client of their employer. The construction site was without electricity and deliveries of construction materials from Sweden ceased. No pressure was being put on the Latvian employer to become a member of a Swedish employers' organisation. With the exception of a minor incident which lasted for about ten minutes, the Latvian workers were free to enter and leave the construction site.

As a result of the blockade, construction work ended on the building site. Baltic Bygg became the subject of liquidation proceedings. Laval, the parent company, started legal proceedings at the Stockholm *Arbetsdomstolen* seeking an injunction to stop the collective action and asking for compensation for the loss it had suffered.

5.2.4. Distinctions between Laval and Viking

Both cases affect the relationship between the right to take collective action and the Free Movement principles. However, when taking a closer look some striking differences also appear.

Laval affected the construction sector, whereas *Viking* affected the maritime sector. Workers active in both industries did not enjoy the same protection in the case of restructuring. Whereas employers in the maritime sector were effectively covered by a specific Regulation relating to their freedom to provide services[83], they were not affected by EC Directives guaranteeing workers' involvement and employment protection in cases of restructuring. Thus, neither the Collective Redundancies Directive, nor the Acquired Rights Directive is applicable to the maritime sector.[84] For this reason, the observation by Maduro in his *Viking* opinion that EC Law "does not turn a blind eye to the workers who are adversely affected by the negative traits of the Common Market"[85] is fallacious. EC Law does explicitly turn a blind eye to workers on seagoing vessels. The latter is astonishing, since an outsourcing operation as shown by *Viking* is much easier to operate. Insofar as it is being operated by a reflagging operation, it boils down to mere legal operations. Chaumette has argued that it could be operated within 24 hours.[86] For that reason, the idea raised by Advocate General Maduro to bifurcate between legitimate boycotts prior to relocation and illegitimate collective action posterior to relocation is problematic.[87]

In *Laval* and *Viking*, trade unions resorted to boycott actions. However, there is a major difference between the boycotts concerned. Boycotts can be characterized as actions undertaken by economic actors (workers and/or unions) not having a (direct) contractual relationship with an enterprise and which are detrimental to the proper functioning of that enterprise. The workers will be engaged in an action which is not directed against *their* employer. Boycotts can cover distinct strategies. The oldest recorded type of boycott action is the refusal to conclude

83 See EC Regulation 4055/86.

84 See Directive 98/59 (Article 1 2) c) (crews of seagoing vessels and 2001/23); Article 1 3) (The crew of seagoing vessels) Acquired Rights Directive 2001/23.

85 See the opinion of AG Maduro in *Laval*, §59.

86 P. Chaumette, (2008), 216.

87 See the opinion of Maduro in *Viking*, §§64–68.

employment contracts with an employer which is blacklisted (*mise à l'index, interdiction*). It predates the development of the strike as a collective abstention from contracted work. This technique was often used by Journeymen associations (les *compagnonnages*) in the *Ancien Régime*.[88] Basically, this type of boycott can be described as a collective exercise of the individual freedom (not) to work. Since all employees have the freedom not to conclude contracts of employment, it is difficult to imagine how the collective exercise of such a right might be unlawful. The difference with strike actions is obvious. The isolated refusal by an individual to perform his contract of employment will often constitute a breach of contract. The collective exercise of this action will be a necessary prerequisite for its qualification as a lawful action. The infamous *Loi le Chapelier* did contain an express provision prohibiting such boycotts. In French various expressions are used, among which is the term "circulaire". The similarity with the practice of "circulars" being issued by the ITF is obvious. In so far as unions call for such a boycott, their actions are not covered by the freedom to work. However, their appeal to workers can be qualified as the exercise of their freedom of expression.

A more frequent type of boycott is the refusal of workers to perform their contract of employment for the benefit of certain *clients* of their employer that are being blacklisted. The refusal of dockers to load or unload ships under a flag of convenience constitutes a classic example. Boycott actions will not *per se* be qualified as strike actions. In a classic approach, a strike presupposes a total refusal to perform the contract of employment. A selective refusal to perform certain tasks might not be considered to constitute strike action.

In so far as the employer will not instruct the workers to perform their contract of employment for the benefit of other clients, the boycott action will qualify as a strike action. In the latter case, the strike will often constitute a solidarity action. The collective actions undertaken in *Laval* constitute an example of this second type of boycott action. Thus, the Swedish trade unions called for a boycott of Laval's construction site and they effectively precluded access to electricity. However, the Court of Justice tended to refer to the actions in Laval primarily as blockade actions.[89] These actions are of a different nature. They presuppose that members of a picket effectively prohibited Latvian workers from having access to the site and that they prevented vehicles from entering the site. This version of the facts does not coincide at all with the way in which the facts were indicated in the referring judgement of the *Arbetdomstolen* of 29 April 2005. The Swedish Labour Court only mentioned the existence of two minor incidents. On 12 November 2004 a truck was requested not to deliver goods to the plant. After comments and

88 For a historical analysis: C. Lis and H. Soly, "An irresistible Phalanx: Journeymen Associations in Western Europe 1300–1800", [1994] *International Review of Social History*, 11–52.

89 *Laval* judgement, §34 and §107.

inquiries by Laval, the delivery finally took place some days later. Another incident occurred on 13 December 2004. About 50 members of Byggnads blocked the entrance used by the Latvian workers and intimidated them. The incident did not last for longer than ten minutes. The qualification of the entire collective action which lasted for several weeks as a blockade is therefore misleading. It is not corroborated by the facts of the case as they were examined by the referring judge. In general, the attitude of the pickets surrounding the Laval site hence needs to be considered as the exercise of the freedom of peaceful assembly.[90] The presence of strike pickets was primarily intended to communicate the policy of the trade union and to persuade the posted workers to go home.

In *Laval* and *Viking* solidarity strikes lay at the heart of the dispute. ITF expressed its solidarity by issuing a circular. In the same vein, the Swedish trade union expressed its solidarity with the posted workers who were deprived of the benefit of a level of wages which is customary on the Swedish Labour Market. In *Viking*, the solidarity action by ITF was a secondary action, which was issued subsequent to the notification of the FSU to call for a strike. The employees concerned were involved in the collective action. The action which had been notified by FSU was a primary action.[91] In *Laval*, the posted workers were not involved in any strike action. The solidarity boycott of the Swedish unions can hardly be qualified as a secondary action. It did constitute a solidarity strike *sui generis*. It is obvious that the solidarity strike was not entirely "altruistic". It sought to safeguard the interests of all the workers active on Swedish soil.

Furthermore, the question arises to what extent the collective action in *Laval* can be qualified as a cross-border collective action. From a formal and legalistic point of view, it affected two distinct workforces which were allocated on to the Swedish and the Latvian labour market. From a trade union perspective, the collective action only related to all the workers who were active on Swedish soil in the construction sector. The Swedish trade union movement contested the artificial partitioning of workers active on Swedish soil into two labour markets.

In both cases collective bargaining lay at the heart of the issue. In *Viking*, ITF sought to prevent the shipowner from concluding a collective agreement with a non-Finnish Union. However, in *Laval* the Swedish Unions tried to force a Latvian company to conclude a tie-in agreement. Furthermore, in *Viking* the employer sought to prohibit a collective action *ad futurum* which had not yet been undertaken by the Finnish trade union. Insofar as legal action was undertaken against an existing ITF "circular", the question arose whether the formal

90 See Arbetsdomstolen Stockholm, Case A 268/04, 29 April 2005.
91 T. Novitz (2006), p. 244.

withdrawal of such a circular would effectively have an impact on the attitude of its affiliates. In essence, the circular seems to have been of a declaratory nature clarifying, in a concrete case, the implications of the FOC. The obligation to respect that campaign did not stem from the circular, but from affiliation to the ITF. These "obligations" are as autonomous as the affiliation of the trade unions to the ITF. The distinction that Maduro suggested in his *Viking* opinion between an autonomous or voluntary co-ordinated action of national trade unions and a transnational collective action that flows from a membership's obligation is puzzling to say the least. Contracted obligations are autonomous and voluntary as well. The idea that a circular action could constitute a "collective action" is puzzling. Bercusson[92] rightly pointed out that ITF could not have any recourse to collective action. The refusal to conclude a collective agreement with the blacklisted employer would in fact be operated through their affiliates. In the same vein, it is worth reminding that insofar as boycott actions and strike actions are related to the conclusion and/or performance of individual employment contracts, trade unions are not engaged in collective actions. The refusal to conclude or to perform an employment contract can only be carried out by individual employees. The question whether merely calling for this kind of action, *id est* exercising the freedom of expression, should be prohibited is worth considering. It seems to be based on a vicious organic and militaristic conception of collective action which downgrades employees from citizens to automatons.

Last but not least, *Laval* dealt with the issue of the Freedom to provide Services, whereas in *Viking* the freedom of establishment was at issue. Since the labour law issues of the Freedom to Provide Services are dealt with in the Posting of Workers Directive, the *Laval* issues raise a question regarding the relationship between the PWD and primary EC Law.

6. A HERMENEUTICAL FRAMEWORK TO COPE WITH *LAVAL* AND *VIKING*

6.1. TACKLING AN ANTINOMY

In *Laval* and *Viking*, the Court was invited to assess an alleged ***antinomy*** between a fundamental economic freedom and a fundamental right. The alleged antinomy can only be situated *within* Community Law, insofar as both conflicting legal principles concerned are part of the same legal order (see 6.5). Furthermore, the fundamental freedoms concerned need to apply to the facts (see 6.2) of the case

92 B. Bercusson, (2007), 304–305.

and their nature needs to warrant the conclusion that the applicant in the proceedings before the referring judge can effectively invoke fundamental freedoms against the defendant by pretending to have exercised his fundamental right to have recourse to collective action (see 6.3). Last but not least, an antinomy only exists insofar as it could be claimed that the collective action did in fact restrict the freedom to provide services (see 6.4). If these conditions are fulfilled, the Court is forced to tackle the *antinomy* either by establishing a clear-cut hierarchy or by engaging in a balancing operation (see 6.6).

In *Laval* the question is even more complex, since the right to take collective action was said to conflict with a legal standard of primary EC Law as well as with an instrument of secondary EC Law, *i.e.* the Posting of Workers Directive 96/71.

In *Laval,* the Court was also asked to examine to what extent the *Lex Brittania* was compatible with the prohibition of discrimination against foreign Service Providers.[93]

Under the *Lex Brittania* a collective action against a service provider who is bound by a collective agreement was considered to be illegitimate, unless that service provider was bound by a non-Swedish collective agreement. The Court recognised that the *Lex Brittania* treats foreign service providers who had concluded a (non-)Swedish agreement in the same way as a Swedish employer who had *not* concluded any agreement at all. By submitting foreign service providers to the same rules as a Swedish employer in a different situation, the *Lex Brittania* failed to pass the non-discrimination test. The Court was unable to detect the existence of any grounds related to public policy, public security or public health within the meaning of Article 46 TEC to justify such discrimination.[94]

For two reasons the second question does not relate as such to the conflict between the right to take collective action and the freedom to provide services. It focuses on the issue whether Member States have the freedom to protect collective actions in a way which is discriminatory *vis-à-vis* foreign service providers. Contrary to the other issues involved in *Viking* and *Laval,* it does not as such directly restrict the freedom of trade unions, since it is addressed to Member States regulating the right to take collective action. Hence, it does not impose any obligation on the trade unions concerned. In practice, trade unions might be confronted with the problem that their actions cannot be protected by invoking domestic law which is held to be discriminatory towards EC Law. The Court did not answer how this discrimination needs to be resolved. In our view, the discrimination could be

93 See Article 46 in conjunction with Article 49 TEC.

94 *Laval* judgement §115–120.

lifted not by prohibiting all collective actions which are directed against an employer which is bound by a collective agreement, but rather by excluding any *statutory* prohibition on having recourse to collective action on the ground that the employer is bound by a collective agreement. A less drastic solution could be to reformulate the *Lex Brittania* by stating "that an industrial action is unlawful if it aims to replace or alter an existing collective agreement, if that collective agreement prescribes at least the same level of protection as the collective agreement concluded by the most representative employers' and labour organisations at the national level".[95] Another solution might be to restrict the prohibiting effect of a peace obligation to the trade unions who have actually signed the collective agreement.[96] This solution differs from the first solution which we envisaged insofar as the latter tends to consecrate a doctrine of implied peace obligations in a statutory way. In our view, only the first solution will protect the Swedish system from a more important criticism. Article 6 §4 of the European Social Charter allows for restrictions on collective actions if they are *enshrined* in a collective agreement. It is far from obvious that this article allows for restrictions laid down in a law which refers to the existence of a collective agreement in order to restrict the right to take collective action by certain persons, irrespective of whether or not they are signatory parties to that agreement. In other words, it should be beyond doubt that peace obligations do reflect the will of the signatory parties.[97]

In sum, the Court had various ways to circumvent the assessment of the alleged antinomy.

It could have argued that the free movement principles *do not apply* to the collective actions concerned (the *Albany avenue*). It could have argued that employers could not invoke the principles regarding the freedom to provide services and the freedom of establishment against private organisations such as trade unions (the issue of horizontal effect). The Court might have questioned whether the collective actions concerned did indeed restrict both freedoms. Instead the Court did recognise that both freedoms were applicable to the facts of the case. It determined that employers could invoke them against trade unions engaged in the collective actions concerned. It recognised that there was an

95 In this sense: K. Ahlberg, N. Bruun, and J. Malmberg, "The *Vaxholm* case from a Swedish and European perspective", [2006] 2, *Transfer* 165–166. It is however questionable whether such a formula would pass the test of conformity with regard to the Posting of Workers Directive in conjunction with Article 49 TEC as it is interpreted by the Court of Justice.

96 T. Van Peijpe, (2008), pp 182–183.

97 In this respect, see: European Committee on Social Rights; Digest of the case law, p 72. www.coe.int/t/e/human_rights/esc/7_Resources/Digest_en.pdf:
"The systems of industrial relations in which collective agreements are seen as a social peace treaty during which strikes are prohibited are in conformity with Article 6§4. However, a peace obligation must reflect with certainty the will of social partners."

antinomy within the same legal order by recognising the right to collective action as a general principle of Community law. Instead of establishing a clear-cut hierarchy between the conflicting principles, the Court decided that the conflict needed to be tackled on the basis of the assessment whether a fair balance had been struck. In *Viking* such a test was merely prescribed for the benefit of the referring judge. In *Laval*, the Court decided to dictate the outcome of the test to the referring judge.

The judgements of both Courts will be analysed on the basis of the hermeneutic framework described above. Since the focus of the research is concentrated on the relationship between these two conflicting principles, the legal niceties surrounding the interpretation of the PWD and its implementation in Sweden and the *Lex Brittania* will be treated in a functional manner. In the same vein, this contribution does not endeavour to provide an in-depth analysis of the Posting of Workers Directive as such.

6.2. THE REJECTION OF THE *ALBANY* AVENUE

In *Albany* the Court determined "that agreements concluded in the context of collective negotiations between management and labour in pursuit of the general objectives enshrined in the introductory provisions as well as in the specific provisions related to social policy must, by virtue of their nature and purpose, be regarded as falling outside the scope of Article 85(1) of the Treaty."[98] *Mutatis mutandis*, the *Albany* precedent could have urged the Court to avoid an antinomy between the right to take collective action and the fundamental freedoms concerned by stating that the Treaty provisions in question did not apply to the collective actions in *Viking* and *Laval*. The Court of Justice refused to adopt the Albany avenue.

The Court explicitly stated that the collective actions under scrutiny neither fell outside Article 43 TEC (Freedom to provide services) nor outside Article 49 TEC (Freedom of Establishment).[99] In *Viking*, the Court answered the preliminary question of the Court of Appeal requesting the Court of Justice to consider its previous recitals in *Albany*. Both the ITF and the FSU argued that there was a clear-cut analogy with Albany. In *Laval*, the Court had to respond to an argument which was raised by the Swedish trade unions as defendants in the main proceeding and by the Danish and Swedish Governments in their submissions. No explicit link with *Albany* was raised in the preliminary questions. Furthermore, the argument was construed on the basis of a provision precluding any legislative

[98] *Albany* judgment, §60.
[99] *Viking* judgement, §55 and *Laval* judgment, §94–95.

competence to intervene in the field of collective action under the Social Policy Treaty Provisions.

The Court rejected both arguments to construe an exemption for collective actions from the Freedom of Establishment and the Freedom to Provide services. It refuted the existence of any similarity with the so-called exemption from competition rules for collective agreements. In *Albany* the exemption was considered to be necessary in order to prevent the social policy objectives pursued by collective agreements from being seriously undermined. In order to establish that necessity, the court considered that "certain restrictions of competition are inherent in collective agreements between organisations representing employers and workers."[100]

In *Viking*, the Court rejected the idea that there was *an inherent contradiction* between collective actions and fundamental freedoms. It stated that it cannot be considered that it is inherent in the very exercise of trade union rights and the right to take collective action that those fundamental freedoms will be prejudiced to a certain degree.[101]

In *Laval*, the Court convincingly demonstrated that a provision related to EC competences in the field of Social Policy could not have any bearing on the relation between collective action and the Treaty Provisions related to the Freedom to provide services. Neither could the nature of the right to take collective action warrant the conclusion that collective actions fall outside the scope of Article 49.[102]

AG Maduro was very explicit in his condemnation of the *Albany* doctrine.[103] Maduro referred to the judgement, whereas Mengozzi was astonishingly silent on that judgement in his opinion and in the subsequent footnotes. Both Advocates General wondered about the question whether the relevant economic principles are applicable to the right to take collective action. Maduro examined whether the assertion that these principles are not applicable can be validated. He explicitly referred to the *Albany* doctrine as the doctrine of "anti-trust immunity".[104] In our view Albany did not grant an immunity in the technical meaning of the term. An immunity presupposes the application of relevant competition rules, from which collective agreements are exempted or immunized. The Court stated in *Albany*

100 *Albany* judgement, §59.
101 *Viking* judgement, §51–52.
102 *Laval* judgement, §95.
103 See the Opinion of AG Maduro in *Viking*, §26–27.
104 See the Opinion of AG Maduro in *Viking*, §26.

that these provisions fall outside the scope of competition rules, hence they *do not apply*. An immunity boils down to the notion that rules *do not affect* a phenomenon which is being exempted. The difference between both expressions is mirrored by the clause in the *Monti* Regulation 2679/98 and by the distinction in the Services Directive 2006/123 between "not apply" and "not affect".[105]

The Monti Regulation constitutes the proper way of immunising phenomena, without altering the fact that the principles of the EC instruments do apply. A comparison between the *Monti* Regulation and the *Schmidberger* judgement suggests that proper immunisation from the four freedoms needs to be constitutionnally anchored. It cannot be solely based upon secondary Community Law. The *formula* of the Services Directive provides evidence of such an assessment.[106]

Maduro and the Court of Justice argued that there is no analogy between *Albany* and the facts of the case. In my view, however, the analogy is obvious. *Albany seeks* to protect the freedom of collective bargaining, despite its silence the recognition of such a freedom as a general principle of EC law. The *effet utile* of the *Albany* 'immunity' would be seriously undermined if the avenue towards the conclusion of these agreements would be hampered by the prohibition of collective action. The argument which Maduro raised *could* have been seriously corroborated by making a distinction between competition rules and the free movement rules. In this respect, free movement can be said to have been upgraded to the status of a fundamental right. The Nice Charter unfortunately provides proof of such an assessment. It blurs the distinction which the European Constitution has made between fundamental rights and fundamental freedoms.[107] However, Maduro's approach consistently tends to downgrade free movement as an aspect of Common Market Policy. A clue to understanding the lack of an analogy might be Maduro's assessment that, in order to follow the *Albany* avenue, there should be a *logical contradiction* between the social objectives and the freedom of establishment. In this respect competition and collective bargaining can be seen as irreconcilable. Another clue to understanding the lack of an analogy with *Albany* is related to the consideration of the Court in *Albany* that the EC Treaty explicitly promotes social dialogue.[108] The observation was not entirely convincing, however. The TEC stimulates social dialogue at a European level, whereas the social dialogue in *Albany* was at a national branch level. The fact remains that the EC Treaty is silent

105 See Articles 1 and 2 Services Directive.
106 See Article 1 6) Services Directive: "in accordance with national law which respects Community law".
107 See Article 15 of the Nice Charter.
108 See *Albany* judgment, §56.

about collective action. It is explicitly silent by refuting any EC competence in the field of social policy to regulate on that issue.[109]

The approach adopted by the Court and Advocate General Maduro to assess the relationship between collective action and fundamental freedom is entirely artificial and scholastic. They tend to assess that relation in a conceptual manner, on the basis of a logical analysis *a priori* of both concepts. In our view, such an approach needs to be complemented by a proper or synthetic understanding of industrial relations. From that perspective, collective bargaining and collective action are intertwined phenomena. In fact, the Court provides proof of its intellectual ability to engage in such an approach. The Court has recognised that they are intertwined.[110] It explicitly acknowledged the observations by FSU and ITF in that regard. This was done in order to defend the view that Article 43 TEC could be invoked by an employer against these trade unions.[111]

In our view, the fact that they are *inextricably* linked constitutes an argument in favour of applying the *Albany* avenue to the present case. Indeed, it is useless to safeguard the freedom of collective bargaining from the legal niceties of Competition rules when the *via aurea* for the conclusion of a collective agreement, *id est* the collective action, is being blocked.

The distinction between competition and free movement/establishment is artificial as well. Both concepts are relevant for the establishment and the functioning of the Common Market.

The situation can easily be illustrated by the facts in *Albany*. In this case a collective agreement was concluded regarding supplementary pension schemes that severely restricted the choice of the pension fund concerned. The Court was aware that the agreement by its very nature was able to restrict free competition.[112]

---

109 See Article 137 5) TEC.

110 See *Viking* judgement, §36 in conjunction with §60–61.

111 See *verbatim* §36 of the *Viking* judgement: "Secondly, as FSU and ITF submit, collective action such as that at issue in the main proceedings, which may be the trade unions' last resort to ensure the success of their claim to regulate the work of Viking's employees collectively, must be considered to be inextricably linked to the collective agreement the conclusion of which FSU is seeking."

112 See §§48–50 of the *Albany* judgment:
"48 First, by entrusting the operation of a compulsory scheme to a single manager, it deprives the undertakings operating in the sector concerned of the possibility of affiliation to another pension scheme managed by other insurers. Second, that agreement excludes the latter insurers from a substantial part of the pension insurance market.
49 The effects of such an agreement on competition are 'appreciable' because it affects the entire Netherlands textile sector. They are aggravated by the cumulative effect of making affiliation to pension schemes compulsory in numerous sectors of the economy and for all undertakings in those sectors.

It is obvious from these agreements that they are able to restrict the Freedom to Provide Services as well. Insofar as the reasoning in *Laval* and *Viking* will preclude a collective action forcing an employer to conclude such an agreement, the so-called "immunity" from competition rules granted to collective agreements seems to be deprived of its *effet utile*. *Viking* and *Laval* will effectively preclude the ability of trade unions to conclude such a collective agreement. In our view, the reasoning of the Court that not all collective actions will be prejudicial to fundamental freedoms of establishment and the freedom to provide services is valid. It is far from helpful. The fact remains that some collective actions, in order to prevent social dumping, do generate inherent restrictions on the freedom of establishment and the freedom to provide services as construed by the Court. In fact, Vigneau has argued that collective actions such as blockades, irrespective of their aims, tend to obstruct the freedom to provide services.[113] The prohibition of these collective actions inevitably undermines the social policy objectives of the European Union.

According to Maduro, *Schmidberger* needs to be construed as a formal rejection of the *Albany* approach.[114] This assertion can be questioned, since the *Albany* approach has been backed by other judgements of the Court, like *Drijvende Bokken* or *Van der Woude*. The Court of Justice in fact upholds the *Albany* judgement. It refuses to accept the idea that it has been overruled by the later *Schmidberger* judgement. The *Albany* avenue is rejected for a different reason. The Court merely distinguishes and refutes an extrapolation *per analogiam*.

6.3. EMPLOYERS INVOKING ARTICLES 43 AND 49 AGAINST TRADE UNIONS

The Court of Justice refutes the idea that the provisions related to the freedom of establishment could not be invoked by Viking against the collective actions undertaken by ITF and FSU.[115] In *Laval* and *Viking*, the Court explicitly considered that the abolition of obstacles to the Freedom of establishment and the Freedom to Provide Services would be compromised if the abolition of State barriers could

50 Moreover, such an agreement affects trade between Member States in so far as it concerns undertakings which engage in cross-frontier business and deprives insurers established in other Member States of the opportunity to offer a full pension scheme in the Netherlands either by virtue of cross-frontier services or through branches or subsidiaries".

113 C. Vigneau (2008), p 35.

114 See §24 of the Opinion of AG Maduro.

115 See *Viking* judgement, §§56–66.

be neutralised by obstacles resulting from the exercise of "their legal autonomy by associations or organisations not governed by public law".[116]

Hence, according to the Court, the collective actions under scrutiny were qualified as an exercise of *legal autonomy* by trade unions which in fact created an obstacle to the exercise of the freedom of establishment and the freedom to provide services. The collective actions were said to make the exercise of these fundamental freedoms less attractive or more difficult. However, the Court has refused to state generally that these provisions have a direct horizontal effect. Instead, it has referred to existing case law stating that *in casu* there was a functional similarity between some private actors and public law bodies insofar as the first did produce "rules which are not public in nature, but which are designed to regulate, collectively the provision of services".[117]

Astonishingly, the assertion has been based on the desire to safeguard the *effet utile* of the prohibitions imposed upon Member States to obstruct the freedom of establishment and the freedom to provide services. In our view, there is no pressing need to assume that Articles 43 and 49 TEC have such a horizontal effect. In line with *Spanish Strawberries* and *Schmidberger* a victim can always address the Member State due to its omission to intervene against private individuals obstructing the freedom of establishment. Furthermore, in our view the existing case law[118] to which the Court referred to, deals with private parties exercising regulatory competences. In this case, however, the collective action by ITF primarily served to *prevent* any non-Finnish Union from exercising regulatory competences. Furthermore, there is a clear-cut distinction between the exercise of regulatory functions (which can be powers delegated by the government or autonomous powers recognised by the government) and the exercise of the right to take collective action. The difference is intertwined with the difference between legal acts and purely material acts. The Court considered that there is no indication that could validly support that its pre-existing case[119] law regarding fundamental freedoms would only apply to associations or to organisations exercising a regulatory task or having quasi-legislative powers.[120] Hence, the Court distinguished the exercise of legal autonomy as a generic concept from the *species* of the exercise of a regulatory task or of quasi-legislative powers. The conclusion

116 See *Laval* judgement, §98 and *Viking* §57.

117 See *Laval* judgement, §98.

118 Existing case law: ECJ, C-36/74 (*Walrave and Koch);* ECJ (Bosman), C-415/93; ECJ, C-309/99 (*Wouters and Others*).

119 For an analysis of the issue of horizontal effect related to fundamental freedoms: P. Oliver and W.H. Roth, "The internal Market and the Four Freedoms", [2004], *Common Market Law Review,* p. 421–429 and C. Barnard (2007), pp. 179–180.

120 See *Viking* judgement, §65.

of private law agreements to regulate paid work collectively is distinguished from the exercise of a regulatory task. The distinction is crucial since the degree to which collective bargaining has been moulded within a public law framework can be divergent among the Member States. However, the Court did not argue the opposite view that the freedom of establishment and the freedom to provide services could be invoked against any obstacle at all stemming from an association or organisation. Instead the Court required that the obstacle can be legally construed as the exercise of "legal autonomy" conferred on these private law entities by the State. However, it has failed to indicate how the exercise of the right to take collective action can be construed as the exercise of "legal autonomy". Collective action basically boils down to the exercise of economic power, which is essentially different from the exercise of legal autonomy.

A comparison of the judgements with the opinions of Advocates General Maduro and Mengozzi reveals that the Court refused to entertain the thesis that articles 43 and 49 can be considered to have a fully-fledged horizontal effect. Both Advocates General defended the more far-reaching idea that the freedom of establishment and the freedom to provide services have a horizontal effect. Mengozzi clearly refuted the notion that there is an analogy between trade unions engaged in collective actions and bodies producing "regulations" and "rules".[121] He clearly indicated that he was aware of the fact that he was extrapolating from regulatory powers by finding that any compelling obstacle whatsoever was an obstacle to free movement.[122] Maduro seemed to underestimate this essential distinction in his opinion.[123] The opinion is problematic from another point of view as well. In his analysis, he focused on the necessity to acknowledge the horizontal effect vis-à-vis *undertakings* as market participants.[124] The approach of trade unions as market participants, let alone undertakings, is indeed questionable.[125]

The assessment of the Court is far from obvious. The nature of collective actions as the exercise of legal autonomy is puzzling. Davies has argued that the issue is not about the exercise of regulatory power, but rather of economic power.[126] In sum, the Court seems to confuse the process of collective bargaining, which could

121 See the Opinion of AG Mengozzi in *Laval*, §158.
122 See the Opinion of AG Mengozzi in *Laval*, §137.
123 See the Opinion of AG Maduro in *Viking* §45.
124 See the Opinion of AG Maduro in *Viking*, §34.
125 In this respect see the critical observations by P. Oliver and W.H. Roth, "The internal Market and the Four Freedoms", [2004], *Common Market Law Review*, 423. Both authors stress the historical relationship between the four freedoms and competition rules. The latter are applicable solely to undertakings.
126 A.C.L. Davies, (2006), p. 80. In the same vein, S. Robin-Olivier and E. Pataut, (2008), p. 85.

be viewed as the exercise of legal autonomy, with the right to take collective action. In *Viking,* the "collective action" cannot be associated with the exercise of legal autonomy. The conflict between Laval and the ITF touches upon the refusal to exercise legal autonomy. However, the Court's assessment that collective bargaining is an example of "legal autonomy *conferred* by the State" is troublesome. It provides evidence of an extremely 'corporatistic' vision of collective bargaining as the outcome of a process of delegation by the State. Indeed, the trade union freedom of collective bargaining is described as a prerogative which is conferred by the State. In our view, freedom of collective bargaining is a fundamental right which is *recognised.* In a contemporary vision of human rights, it is problematic to see such a recognition in terms of a *Charte octroyée.*

The idea that a collective action should be construed as the exercise of legal autonomy as a prerequisite for the "horizontal effect" of the freedom of establishment and the freedom to provide services gives rise to the question of whether wildcat strikes or spontaneous collective actions can be construed as the exercise of legal autonomy. In our view, it is extremely hazardous to construe the exercise of the right to strike by workers as the exercise of legal autonomy. In such a scenario, the instrumental relationship between collective action and a process of collective bargaining which can be related to the exercise of legal autonomy is indeed absent.

6.4. THE ISSUE OF RESTRICTIONS ON FREE MOVEMENT

The alleged antinomy between economic fundamental freedoms and fundamental workers' rights can be resolved insofar as the collective actions concerned can be considered *not* to constitute restrictions on fundamental freedoms. From a formal point of view, only the question whether the freedom of establishment and the freedom to provide services need to be balanced against the right to take collective action is at stake, insofar as the collective actions concerned restrict these freedoms.

In *Laval,* the picture becomes more complicated. The Latvian employer challenged the collective action on the basis of the Posting of Workers Directive in conjunction with Article 49 TEC. The question arises how the Court construed the relation between the assessment of the justified restrictions on the Freedom to provide Services under Article 49 TEC and the obligations stemming from the PWD. The relation that the Court established between the Posting of Workers Directive and the Freedom to Provide Services is troublesome and enigmatic. The Court presented its assessment of the legitimacy of the collective action as a diptych. First, it assessed the legitimacy under the PWD. Than, it continued to assess its legitimacy under Article 49 TEC. Since the separate tests under the PWD and the TEC provisions failed to be positive, the Court did not have to tackle the issue of what would have happened if the collective actions could be justified under the justified restrictions to Article 49 TEC, whereas they failed the test under the PWD.

The opinion of Advocate General Mengozzi is more revealing in this respect. He states that "a measure that is incompatible with Directive 96/71 will, *a fortiori*, be contrary to Article 49 TEC, because that directive is intended, within its specific scope, to implement the terms of that article." He continued by stating that the fact that the collective action meets the PWD test, does not necessarily mean that the latter meets the requirements of Article 49 TEC.[127]

It is doubtful whether the Court followed this line of reasoning. In fact, it established that the collective action was *not* in conformity with the Posting of Workers Directive. Still, it did not deduce from that assessment that it is *a fortiori* incompatible with article 49 TEC. On the contrary, the Court affirmed that it is "necessary to assess from the point of view of Article 49 TEC the collective action".[128] It dedicated 26 paragraphs to that assessment.

In *Wolff Müller*, the Court of Justice gave the impression that conformity with the Posting of Workers Directive does not preclude the necessity to assess the contested domestic measures in the light of Article 49 TEC.[129] In practice, the Court has adopted a pragmatic stance by interpreting the Posting of Workers Directive in the light of Article 49 TEC.

The approach of the Court in *Laval* seems to warrant the interesting prospect that – from a theoretical point of view – non-conformity with the Posting of Workers Directive could be overcome on the basis of the margin offered to Member Sates to restrict the Freedom to Provide Services.[130] This would imply that a violation of the PWD could be overruled insofar as the collective actions can be safeguarded by overriding reasons of public interest which are recognised as legitimate exceptions to the Freedom to Provide Services.

In *Laval,* the Court considered these reasons of public interest by balancing the right to take collective action against Article 49. In doing so, the Court however took fully into account the social protection which was already offered by the PWD.[131]

In *Laval*, the Court recognised that the right to take collective action could *in principle* be exercised for the protection of workers of the Host State against

127 See the Opinion of Mengozzi in *Laval*, §§149–150.
128 See *Laval* judgment, §85.
129 ECJ, C-60/03, 12 October 2004 (*Wolff & Müller*).
130 In this respect, see the observations of T. Van Peijpe, (2008), p. 180–181.
131 See *Laval* judgement, §§107–108.

possible social dumping. Such an exercise could constitute an overriding reason of public interest.[132] In the case at hand the Court rejected the restrictions concerned as being unjustified. The Court assessed the objective of the collective action as excessive and indicated that the restrictions that it entailed were not sufficiently precise and accessible for the service provider.

The issue at stake has an institutional dimension. It is relevant to assess whether secondary EC instruments can restrict the sovereignty of Member States to invoke overriding reasons of public interest. A negative answer needs to be advocated, since it respects the principle of subsidiarity. In this respect, the Community legislator should respect overriding reasons of public interest restricting the freedom to provide services. Insofar as the PWD does not respect this autonomy, it can be considered to be "unconstitutional". This approach deviates from the classic scheme of *Lex specialis derogat lege generali.* In such an approach, the Posting of Workers Directive can be seen as a more concrete provision regarding the freedom to provide services and should overrule the more general principle enshrined in Article 49 TEC. However, such an argument is not conclusive. First, it is questionable in view of the explicit recitals of the EC Directive. More importantly, the *Lex specialis derogat lege generali* can only be applied to instruments of an identical legal nature. Treaty Provisions are superior to secondary Community instruments.

The approach that overriding reasons of public interest, such as the protection of workers, could justify national measures which are a odds with the Posting of Workers Directive was implicitly followed by the Court of Justice in the infamous *Rüffert* case. Interpreting the PWD Directive in the light of Article 49 TEC, the Court did examine whether a violation of the PWD could be justified by the objective of workers' protection. Instead of dogmatically denying such a possibility, the Court argued that the scope and content of the contested domestic measure precluded such a justification. Thus, the Court implicitly indicated that overriding reasons of public interest, such as workers' protection, *could* in a given case justify a violation of the PWD in view of Article 49.[133]

In *Laval* and *Viking* the Court confirmed its attitude of interpreting restrictions on the freedom of establishment and the freedom to provide services in a very broad manner.[134] Any restriction, whether it constitutes discrimination or not, is made subject to judicial scrutiny.

---

132 See *Laval* judgement, §§103 and 107.

133 ECJ, C-346/06, 3 April 2008, §38.

134 See C. Barnard, *The substantive law of the EC*, (Oxford University Press, Oxford, 2004), p. 19, 256–261.

In *Viking* as well as in *Laval,* the Court did *not* entertain the idea that the collective actions under scrutiny constituted discriminatory restrictions on the freedom of establishment as was alleged by Judge Glouster at first instance. In fact, in *Viking* the examination of overriding reasons of public interest implies the opposite. Restrictions which are (directly) discriminatory can only be upheld on grounds of public policy, public security or public health.[135]

Furthermore, the idea that a collective action in order to "force" a service provider to conclude a collective agreement constitutes a restriction on his freedom is highly questionable. From a labour law point of view, obligations stemming from collective agreements need to be construed as self-imposed or autonomous restrictions on the freedom to provide services. If we take a closer look at the PWD, it only deals with collective agreements insofar as these precepts are given a regulatory nature due to State intervention. Such an intervention is described in terms of a decision of a State declaring these agreements universally binding or deciding to base themselves on agreements which are generally applicable.[136] In fact, Article 3(7) of the PWD does not preclude a foreign service provider from applying terms and conditions of employment which are more favourable to workers than those described in the PWD. The Court reduced these provisions to laws or collective agreements in the Member State of origin. The Court acknowledged that the Latvian employer used its freedom of collective bargaining to conclude a collective agreement with a Latvian trade union and to apply the working conditions laid down in such an agreement.[137] The fact that such a collective agreement will often emerge from that trade union's ability to engage in collective action does not constitute a major legal problem. It is incomprehensible why self-imposed or autonomous restrictions based on collective agreements with trade unions from the Host State are to be seen as falling outside the scope of Article 3(7) PWD. *In sum*, the position of the Court provides evidence of the discriminatory attitude of the freedom to collective bargaining on the basis of the nationality of the social partners. According to the Court, the right to conclude a collective agreement in the host state is subject to the condition that the foreign service providers sign these agreements "of their own accord".[138] Hence, the Court distinguished between collective agreements (*sic*) signed "of their own accord" and those which are "forced" subsequent to a collective action. Collective agreements with a trade union of the State of origin are considered to have been concluded "of their own accord". Those that have been concluded with the trade union of the Host State are considered to have been "imposed". From a labour law point of view, such a

135 See Article 46 in conjunction with Article 53 TEC.
136 See Article 3 8) PWD.
137 See *Laval* judgement, §81.
138 See *Laval* judgement §81.

distinction seems to degenerate collective bargaining in the Host Member State with a foreign service provider to collective begging. Thus trade unions tend to be confused with mendicant orders. Such an assessment is insulting both for trade unions as well as for mendicant orders. In fact, the Court tends to operate the very kind of nationality-based discrimination in an area of industrial relations which has urged it to condemn the *Lex Brittania*. The Court seems to leave some room for collective actions in order to enforce the core of mandatory provisions. In some Member States these kinds of collective actions will be considered to fall outside domestic recognition. They do not touch upon a conflict of interest. Furthermore, they cannot be seen as being undertaken by means of an *ultimum remedium,* since a legal action could be said to generate an equivalent effect.

The Court erroneously denied that collective agreements which are concluded due to the exercise of *economic* power need to be construed as self-imposed restrictions. Furthermore, it stated that these agreements cannot be upheld, since Article 3(7) of Directive 96/71 cannot be interpreted as allowing the host member State to make the provision of services conditional upon the observance of terms and conditions of employment which go beyond the mandatory rules for minimum protection.[139] The Court disagreed with the notion that it is not the State but the trade unions which make the provision of services conditional on the observance of these terms and conditions. Insofar as the exercise of collective bargaining is indeed the result of legal autonomy conferred by the State, it needs to be seen as an (implicit) *decision* of the State within the meaning of Article 3(8) of the PWD. Such a decision triggers the application of collective agreements which are generally applicable (though not declared universally applicable).[140]

The attitude of the Court is in fact discriminatory in another aspect. It allows cross-border economic activity for management and it denies cross-border collective action for trade unions. In an era where the Commission is advocating the development of an optional legal framework for transnational collective bargaining[141], the position of the Court is out of date.

6.5. THE RECOGNITION OF THE RIGHT TO TAKE COLLECTIVE ACTION AS A *GENERAL PRINCIPLE*

The judgements in *Laval* and *Viking* constitute landmark decisions insofar as the Court of Justice explicitly recognises the right to take collective action, including

139 See *Laval,* judgement §80.

140 See *Laval* judgement, §67.

141 See COM (2005) 33. Communication from the Commission on the Social Agenda.

the right to strike as a general principle of EC Law. This qualification is based upon international instruments guaranteeing the right to strike which the Member States have signed or co-operated in as well as upon instruments adopted at Community level or within the European Union.[142] In this respect, the Court of Justice explicitly referred to the Charter of Nice. References to the Nice Charter in the case law of the Court of Justice in order to recognise *fundamental workers'* rights are *rari nantes*, not to say non-existent.[143] In another passage, the Court of Justice referred to the case law of the ECHR in order to construe that the right to strike constitutes *an important means* to protect the interests of the members of the trade union. The references to the judgements in *Affaire Syndicat national de la Police belge* and *Wilson* can be complemented by the decision in *Unison* and the judgement in *Dilek*.[144] The two last-mentioned cases tend to affirm that the right to strike is a sufficiently important means to protect workers' rights in order for restrictions to fall under the scrutiny of Article 11 §2 of the ECHR. In practice, such an assessment boils down to the idea that the right to strike is covered by the recognition of the freedom of association. In *Viking*, the Court stressed that "the organisation of collective action by trade unions must be regarded as covered by the legal autonomy which those organisations, which are not public law entities, enjoy pursuant to the trade union rights accorded to them, inter alia by national law".[145] Thus, the Court seems to perceive the right to take collective action as an *accessorium* of the freedom of association.

The Court explicitly considered the reference to the right to take collective action in the European Social Charter signed at Turin on 18 October 1961 and more generally in ILO Convention No. 87 concerning the Freedom of Association and the Protection of the right to organise. Due to the fact that ILO Convention No. 87 does not contain an explicit reference to the right to take collective action nor to the right to strike, the Court thus implicitly confirmed the importance of the *Rechtsfortbildung* developed by the supervisory bodies of the ILO. In fact the FAC has consistently deduced that the right to take collective action is an *accessorium* of the right to organise.[146]

---

142 *Laval* judgement §43, *Viking* judgement, §90.

143 In that respect, see C. Vigneau (2008), II 10060, p. 34 and S. Laulom, "Les actions collectives contre le dumping social", [2008], *Semaine Sociale Lamy*, p 8. For a comprehensive overview on the interpretation of fundamental workers' rights as enshrined in the Nice Charter: B. Bercusson, *European Labour Law and the EU Charter of Fundamental Rights*, (Nomos, Baden-Baden, 2006) 728 p.

144 See *supra* IV B.

145 See *Viking* judgement, §35.

146 In this respect: see International Labour Office Geneva, *Digest of decisions and principles of the Freedom of Association Committee of the Governing Body of the ILO, Freedom of Association*, Fifth (revised) edition, no. 523.

For obvious reasons, the Court has avoided stating that the right to collective action has entered into the common constitutional traditions of the Member States. Recent comprehensive and more restricted comparative overviews have highlighted that the right to take collective action has not been constitutionally anchored in the majority of the Member States. In fact, legal recognition has often flowed from intervention by Supreme Courts.[147]

The Court's approach is consistent with the elabourated views of Mengozzi in his opinion in *Laval*.[148] AG Mengozzi was far more *explicit* in recognising the right to take collective action as a general principle of EC law than Maduro. The latter's recognition of such a general principle is much more implicit. It is implied in the way he rejected the *Albany* approach in favour of the *Schmidberger* approach.[149] He assimilated the fundamental rights approach with the issue of social policy objectives. In his opinion, the recognition of the right to strike seems to be instrumental *vis-à-vis* the recognition of social policy objectives in the EC Treaty. In our view the right to strike needs to be guaranteed in isolation of the EC Treaty's social objectives. Indeed, it flows from common human rights traditions witnessed *inter alia* by the Nice Charter. Maduro tends to make the recognition of the right to take collective action subject to an unwritten social contract which certainly does not flow from common constitutional traditions.[150] His idea that the EC Treaty constitutes a *social contract* is puzzling to say the least. Human Rights as general principles of EC law do not flow from the pseudo-constitutional EC Treaty. They are necessary to protect the citizen against such a Treaty.

Mengozzi's recognition of the right to take collective action deviates from the approach taken by Advocate General Jacobs in his renowned opinion in *Albany* for two reasons. Jacobs recognised that the right to take collective action could be considered to be a general principle insofar as it constitutes a *correlarium* of the freedom of association.[151] Mengozzi seems to favour a recognition of the right to take collective action in its own right. Such an approach is relevant in order to grasp whether EC law recognises the right to strike as an aspect of citizenship (a French and personalistic approach) or in a more 'corporatistic' or organic fashion, which is at odds with the conclusion of the European Committee on Social Rights.

147 F. Dorssemont, (2007), 245–253. For a more comprehensive survey, see W. Warneck, *Strike rules in the EU 27 and beyond*, European Trade Union Institute, Brussels, 2007. www.etui-rehs.org/research/Media/Files/Reports/2007/R103.
148 See the Opinion of AG Mengozzi in *Laval*, §60–78.
149 See the Opinion of AG Maduro in *Viking*, §23 and 24.
150 See the Opinion of AG Maduoro in *Viking*, §§58 and 60.
151 See the Opinion of AG Jacobs, in *Albany*, §159.

Furthermore, Jacobs held that the recognition of general principles requires a "sufficient convergence of national legal orders *and* international legal instruments".[152] A comparative overview of the regulation of the right to strike does not *per se* provide evidence of such a sufficient convergence. Mengozzi did not neglect these divergencies. He made a distinction between the right to resort to collective action and the means of exercising it.[153] He correctly pointed out that in this case the right to take collective action was being exercised in a less universally accepted way, *id est* by a solidarity action and a blockade The question arises how this *obiter dictum* needs to be interpreted. Since the Court can only recognise the right to take collective action as a general principle of EC law, it seems unlikely that a recognition of the solidarity strike and the blockade as general principles of EC Law can ever urge Member States to adapt their regulation on the right to take collective action.

Mengozzi was much more explicit in his recognition of the right to take collective action as a general principle of EC law in its own right. He corroborates this recognition through a detailed extensive analysis of national constitutions and relevant human rights instruments.

In my view, his analysis of the case law regarding article 11 European Convention on Human Rights is outdated and erroneous.[154] Mengozzi stuck to the older case law affirming that the right to take collective action is an important, but not essential means to defend workers' interests.[155]

The distinction that Mengozzi[156] made between the older recognition of the right to strike in Staff cases as a "principle of labour law" and the recognition of the right to strike as a general principle of EC Law is relevant. It indicates that *Laval* and *Viking* constitute landmark judgements.

The question arises whether the recognition of the right to take collective action as a general principle of EC Law has given added value to the debate. Such recognition warrants a discussion on the status of so-called fundamental freedoms *vis-à-vis* that of proper fundamental rights. The language of the Court tends to *downgrade* and *assimilate* these fundamental rights recognised as general principles to the well-known issues of workers' or public interests and of social policy objectives able to restrict fundamental freedoms.[157]

152 See the Opinion of AG Jacobs in *Albany* §160.
153 See the Opinion of AG Mengozzi in *Laval* §80.
154 See the Opinion of AG Mengozzi, §80.
155 See *supra* IV B.
156 See the Opinion of AG Mengozzi §78.
157 See *Viking* judgement, §§75,77, 79. See the *Laval* judgement, §101–103.

Thus the right to collective action is presented as *just* a legitimate interest along the lines of the *Schmidberger* judgement and in keeping with Maduro's observations. The question arises whether the balancing exercise that the Court undertook is essentially different from the way in which other justified restrictions on the freedom of establishment and the freedom to provide services have been formulated and assessed. The latter are related to "overriding reasons of public *intrest*". In our view, the Court does not treat fundamental rights in a different way as a cause for restrictions on fundamental freedoms. It integrates its balancing exercise with respect to fundamental rights and fundamental freedoms within the mould of the case law regarding restrictions on fundamental freedoms based on public interests. A conflict between two values which are incommensurable (*id est,* economic legal principles, such as so-called fundamental freedoms and human rights proper) is thus reduced to a balancing of commensurable "interests".

The Court's approach to the right to take collective actions is progressive insofar as it recognises collective actions which deviate from the classic recourse to strike action. Thus, the Court recognises blockades and solidarity actions. However, it seems to construe the right to take collective action as an *accessorium* to the freedom of association.[158] As indicated *supra*, the Court seemed to deduce the recognition of the right to take collective action primarily from the freedom of association. Such an approach might prove to be detrimental to the recognition of *spontaneous* or *wildcat* strikes. The reference to the European Social Charter allows for an approach in favour of the wildcat strike.[159]

The judgement in *Laval* can be criticised, since the Court refuses to balance the freedom to provide services against another fundamental workers' right which was at stake in *Viking.* ITF appealed to its members to have recourse to the exercise of the negative freedom of collective bargaining. The Court seemed to suggest that the ITF circular, which resulted in the collectively co-ordinated exercise not to engage in collective bargaining, *might* prove to be contrary to the freedom of establishment. Thus, the Court seemed to restrict the negative freedom of collective bargaining. The ITF circular was an extremely "visible" and significant method to exercise that freedom. As indicated earlier, the idea that an extremely civilised and concerted exercise of the negative freedom to contract can be

158 See §35 *Viking* judgement.

159 The European Committee on Social Rights has consistently refused to subordinate the validity of a collective action to the prerequisite that is called for by trade unions. Furthermore, it has been critical about domestic legal orders which do subordinate the validity of the strike to the condition that it has been recognised or organised by a trade union. For a survey: European Committee on Social Rights; Digest of the case law, p. 70. www.coe.int/t/e/human_rights/esc/7_Resources/Digest_en.pdf.

qualified as an illegitimate collective action is reminiscent of the prohibition of coalitions and combinations in the early part of the nineteenth century. It is extremely puzzling to argue that an attitude which is perfectly legitimate if undertaken by a single union will become illegitimate once it is undertaken in a co-ordinated way on a Community-scale level.

6.6. BALANCING FUNDAMENTAL FREEDOMS *VIS-À-VIS* THE RIGHT TO TAKE COLLECTIVE ACTION: PROPORTIONALITY *SUI GENERIS*

The Court of Justice underlined that the recognition of the right to take collective action as a general principle of EC Law will not preclude that it might be made subject to restrictions. The exercise needs to be reconciled with conflicting fundamental freedoms. The Court explicitly indicated that this reconciliation needs to be operated in accordance with the principle of *proportionality*.[160] In our view, the expression "principle of proportionality" refers to a global test. Proportionality *sensu lato* needs to be distinguished from the assessment whether a justified restriction on a fundamental freedom has a proportionate character.[161] The latter is part of the global proportionality test. Thus, the principle of proportionality is applied not to assess restrictions on fundamental rights, but rather on fundamental freedoms. This is a Copernican revolution. According to the Court of Justice, human rights need to be exercised in a moderate way, *id est* in a way which is proportionate to the restrictions which the legal principles of an economic order impose.

The Court referred in this respect to its ruling in *Schmidberger*. However, it is questionable whether *in casibus* the proportionality test is being applied in an identical way.[162]

In *Schmidberger* the Court stated that the desire of the Austrian Republic to safeguard the freedom of expression and the freedom of assembly did constitute a legitimate aim to restrict the free movement of goods. It refused to examine the

160 See *Viking* judgement, §46 and *Laval* judgement, §94.

161 For an identical use of semantics, describing the proportionality test, see B. Caruso "I diritti sociali nello spazio sociale sovranazionale e nazionale: indifferenza, conflitto o integrazione?" (Working papers www.lex.unict.it/eurolabour/ricerca/wp/wp_int.htm).

162 Thus C. Vigneau has indicated that "les arrêts *Viking* et *Laval* parlent de manière beaucoup plus explicite de soumission du droit à l'action collective aux libertés économiques du Traité". The author concludes, however, that the difference in semantics does not upset (bouleverser) the meaning of the cae law of the ECJ. C. Vigneau, (2008), II 10060, p 34. In our view, the Court does apply the principle of proportionality any differently to the right to collective action, as it did in *Schmidberger* with regard to the freedom of expression and the freedom of assembly.

motives underlying the collective actions concerned. In *Viking* and *Laval*, the Court adopted a teleological approach to the fundamental right at stake. Contrary to its doctrine that the protection of human rights is a legitimate interest which in principle justifies a restriction,[163] the Court imposed a teleological condition on that legitimate objective. The Court suggested that the right to take collective action only constitutes a legitimate aim to restrict fundamental freedoms insofar as the exercise of that right serves *the protection of workers' interests*.[164]

Insofar as the human right concerned can be qualified as a quintessential *fundamental* workers' right, this condition seems to be superfluous and redundant at first sight. If we take a closer look, the Court impedes on the autonomous assessment by trade unions and workers regarding their interests. It refuses to accept that it is up to trade unions and workers to assess where their interests lie. The approach of the Court is at odds with a doctrine developed by the Strasbourg European Committee on Social Rights precluding an assessment of the appropriate character of the objectives of trade union actions by the judiciary. The doctrine of the ECSR seeks to restrict the role of the judiciary to a legality test (*jugement de légalité*) as opposed to an appropriateness test (*jugement d'opportunité*).[165]

The *telos* "protection of workers' interests" has been generically formulated. *Ratione personae*, it is broader than the promotion or furtherance of professional relations which affects relations between workers and *their* employers. In *Laval*, the Court recognised that the right to take collective action for the protection of the workers of the *host state* against possible social dumping *may* constitute an overriding reason of public interest.[166] Although this consideration neglects the fact that the collective action was intended to improve the working conditions of the Latvian employees on Swedish soil as well, it has been viewed as an extension of the justified restrictions under previous case law, which primarily focused on the protection of posted workers.[167]

In *Viking* this led the Court of Justice to question the appropriate character of the collective action in some *obiter dicta*. Still, the Court was reluctant. It indicated that it is up to the referring judge to examine these issues further. In *Viking* the

163 See *Laval* judgement §93.

164 See *Viking* judgement, §77 and 80, *Laval* judgement, §103.

165 See the following fragment of the conclusions which have been integrated into the Digest. Conclusions XVII-1, Netherlands, p. 319: "The Committee considers that the fact that a Dutch judge may determine whether recourse to strikes are "premature" impinges on the very substance of the right to strike as this allows the judge to exercise one of the trade unions' key prerogatives, that of deciding whether and when a strike is necessary." Digest of the case law. www.coe.int/t/e/human_rights/esc/7_Resources/Digest_en.pdf.

166 See *Laval* judgement, §103.

167 T. Van Peijpe (2008) p 181.

Court wondered whether there was a serious threat of collective dismissal and of reflagging, in view of the formal statements made by the employer after a strike had been announced by FSU.[168] Furthermore, the Court wondered whether the Flag of Convenience Campaign was in the interests of workers. It was perplexed by the abstract approach of the ITF, which labels the flag of a member State where the ship is not beneficially owned as a flag of convenience, without examining and comparing the labour standards.[169]

In *Laval* the Court seemed to have lost this sense of self-restraint. Although it acknowledged that a collective action in order to combat social conditions for the protection of the workers of the Host State against possible social dumping, may constitute an overriding reason of public interest, it refuted the existence of those reasons in the facts of the present case. The Court considered that the risk of social dumping was sufficiently precluded since the foreign service provider was required, as a result of the co-ordination achieved by the PWD, to observe a nucleus of mandatory rules for minimum protection.[170]

The Court's refusal to acknowledge the very existence of an objective of workers' protection seems to be based on the implicit assumption that the Posting of Workers Directive needs to be construed as a Directive providing for a mandatory maximum level of workers' protection.

In fact, the Court indicated in *Laval,* as well as in *Rüffert,* that Article 3(7) PWD could not be interpreted as allowing the Host State to make the provision of services in its territory conditional on the observance of terms and conditions of employment which go beyond the mandatory rules of "minimum" protection.[171] In this respect, minimum protection boils down to mandatory maximum or standard protection. The *Rüffert* case presents another analogy with the *Laval* case. In *Rüffert* the Court refused to recognise that a law of *Nieder Sachsen* which was explicitly inspired by a desire to combat social dumping and which was in line with the ILO's Labour Clause Convention No. 94 could be considered to serve the objective of workers' protection.[172] This drastic approach of the Court tends to preclude any proper balancing operation *in nuce.*

The Court was obviously aware that this dogmatic and abstract rebuttal could not be entirely convincing as far as the issue of wages is concerned. The facts of the case reveal that the transposition of the PWD was not sufficient to guarantee that

168 See *Viking* judgement, §§80–83.
169 See *Viking* judgement, §89.
170 See *Laval* judgement, §§108.
171 See *Laval* judgement, §80 and see ECJ C-346/06 (*Dirk Rüffert versus Land Niedersachsen*), 3 April 2008, §32–33.
172 ECJ C-346/06 (*Dirk Rüffert versus Land Niedersachsen*), 3 April 2008, §§38–40.

the foreign service provider was bound by any requirement regarding the wages to be paid to the posted workers.

The Court continued to consider the issue of wages more closely. Having considered that the restriction on the fundamental freedom concerned was provoked by pay negotiations of unspecified duration[173], the Court observed that these negotiations were part of a national context characterised by a lack of provisions which are sufficiently precise and accessible in order not to render it impossible or excessively difficult in practice for the service provider to determine the obligations with which it is required to comply as regards minimum pay in that they do not allow it to determine the obligations with which it is required to comply as regards minimum pay.[174]

The Court's insistence on sufficiently precise and accessible restrictions is reminiscent of a discourse regarding the conditions related to human rights restrictions. The Court's reference to this idea provides proof of a tendency to upgrade economic legal freedoms to the status of fully-fledged "human rights".

In doing so, the Court ignored the fact that the restrictions advocated by the Trade Unions and some Member States, *id est* the safeguarding of the right to take collective action, are in fact prescribed by law, *id est* by constitutional traditions and authoritative international instruments. Furthermore, the lack of legal transparency seems to be the result of the obstinate refusal of the foreign service provider to enter into genuine collective bargaining in due time. Furthermore, the Court's insistence on sufficiently precise and accessible restrictions on fundamental freedoms can easily be reversed. According to the ESC, restrictions on the right to collective action need to be prescribed by law as well. The question arises whether the proportionality test prescribed in *Viking* qualifies as such.

The teleological scrutiny of the collective actions concerned deviates from that undertaken by both Advocates General. Mengozzi adopted a more "liberal" and less restrictive approach to the *telos* of collective action.[175] He refused to scrutinize the autonomous assessment regarding the protection of workers' interests. He did however make a distinction between the interest of workers and the 'corporatistic' interest of trade unions. Maduro's teleological restrictions are entirely market-oriented. He tended to subordinate the exercise of collective action to the safeguarding of the Common Market. His opinion mirrors some of the

173 See *Laval* judgement, §101.
174 See *Laval* judgement, §110.
175 See the Opinion of Mengozzi in *Laval,* §212–217.

observations in *Schmidberger* regarding the fact that the ecological activists concerned did not intend to frustrate the free movement of goods.[176]

Advocate General Mengozzi elaborated on the teleological requirements imposed on collective actions in a much more far-reaching way. In our view, Mengozzi thus defended a broad interpretation of the notion of occupational interests in line with the French tradition of interpreting "l'intérêt professionnel". The demarcation which Mengozzi drew is between a trade union's defence of the interests of workers and the 'corporatistic' defence of its proper interests. In this respect, it is clear that some terms of the purported tie-in agreement are considered to be problematic. Mengozzi's assessment was explicitly motivated by the unfavourable assessment of some conditions laid down in a collective agreement which lay at the heart of *Evaldsson*. The ECHR based that judgement on the alleged violation of property rights.[177] Mengozzi indicated that the hard core of collective agreements, such as *Tarifverträge* fixing a rate of pay, will not in principle be compromised by the necessity to respect Article 49 EC Treaty.[178]

For Mengozzi, the teleological restriction on the right to take collective action needs to be assessed in a different way. He generally accepted that collective actions undertaken to defend and protect workers' interests are legitimate. He indicated that this *formula* needs to be broadly interpreted. He stated: "In that regard, although the order for reference is not particularly explicit, the national court mentions, among the aims underlying the collective action taken, the protection of workers and the fight against social dumping. Those two aims might seem to go beyond the scope of the purpose of trade union activity, which in principle is to defend the occupational interests of its own members. However, that fact is no reason for disregarding the possibility that collective action taken by trade unions, of the kind at issue in this case, might truly be directed towards the two abovementioned aims".[179]

In our view, the Court distanced itself from the restrictive attitude that Maduro developed to legitimate goals for collective actions. In this respect, the assessment is more in line with that undertaken by Mengozzi in his opinion on *Laval*.

Maduro stated that "collective action that has the effect of partitioning the labour market and that impedes the hiring of seafarers from certain Member States in order to protect the jobs of seafarers in other Member States would strike at the

176 See *Schmidberger* judgement, §86.
177 See ECHR, 13 February 2007, no. 75252/01 (*Evaldsson and others versus Sweden*). For a comment: F. Dorssemont, [2007] *European Human rights cases*, 474–477.
178 See the Opinion of AG Mengozzi in *Laval*, §245.
179 See the Opinion of Mengozzi in *Laval*, §§246–248.

heart of the principle of non-discrimination on which the common market is founded".[180]

Maduro described two scenarios which would lead to such a partitioning of the labour market. He argued: "A collective action that merely seeks to prevent an undertaking that has moved elsewhere from lawfully providing its services in the Member State in which it was previously established" is considered to partition the labour market.[181] Furthermore, he indicated that "a policy of coordinated collective action could easily be abused in a discriminatory manner if it operated on the basis of an obligation imposed on all national unions to support collective action by any of their fellow unions. It would enable any national union to summon the assistance of other unions in order to make relocation to another Member State conditional on the application of its own preferred standards of worker protection, even after relocation has taken place. In effect, therefore, such a policy would be liable to protect the collective bargaining power of some national unions at the expense of the interests of others, and to partition the labour market in breach of the rules on freedom of movement".[182]

Maduro also contemplated a second scenario. It deals with a collective action allegedly undertaken to improve the terms of employment of seafarers throughout the Community which he considered could create a risk of partitioning the labour market. He stated that "a policy of coordinated collective action could easily be abused in a discriminatory manner if it operated on the basis of an obligation imposed on all national unions to support collective action by any of their fellow unions. It would enable any national union to summon the assistance of other unions in order to make relocation to another Member State conditional on the application of its own preferred standards of worker protection, even after relocation has taken place. In effect, therefore, such a policy would be liable to protect the collective bargaining power of some national unions at the expense of the interests of others, and to partition the labour market in breach of the rules on freedom of movement".[183]

The question arises to which labour market Maduro was referring to. At first sight, it seems obvious to imagine a European labour market. The question arises whether such a labour market exists at all. In our view the fragmentated state of European Labour Law, *a fortiori* the lack of any competence of the EC to regulate with regard to the remuneration of labour under the Social Policy Title, amounts to the conclusion that no European Labour market exists. In fact, there are as

180 See the Opinion of Maduro in *Viking* §62.
181 See the Opinion of Maduro in *Viking*, §67.
182 See the Opinion of Maduro in *Viking*, §71.
183 See the Opinion of Maduro in *Viking*, §71.

many labour markets as there are Member States. The principle of the free movement of workers suggests that all workers should have access to domestic labour markets. The reference to labour markets is puzzling since *Laval* and *Viking* do *not* deal with the free movement of workers. In our view, neither the Finnish nor the Swedish union contested the fact that Estonian or Latvian citizens should have access to the Finnish or the Swedish labour markets. The issue is whether service providers should respect the labour standards that are applicable to these domestic markets. Their revindications in fact serve to *prevent* the partitioning of the Finnish and the Swedish labour market, irrespective of the nationality of the workers.

One might argue that *Laval* and *Viking* constitute two distinct scenarios. In *Laval* the Latvian company exercised its freedom of establishment and was effectively recruiting workers from Latvia. In *Viking*, that company was said to be prevented from establishing itself in Estonia. Subsequently, the Estonian subsidiary was confronted with a *partitioned* Estonian labour market. To some workers active on the Estonian labour market, Estonian wages would apply. To other workers employed for an activity formerly undertaken on the Finnish labour market, Finnish labour standards would be enforced. In our view, the industrial dispute in *Laval* is more about the *identification* of the relevant labour market, than about the partitioning of that market. ITF's policy sought to identify the labour market in the function of the company which beneficially owned the *Rosella*. ITF disputed the fact that the flag of convenience was a relevant criterion to identify that labour market.

The distinctions made by Maduro are not deprived of ambiguity.[184] In the first forbidden scenario, the question arises how to date the operation described as relocation. Does this concept refer to a legal or a factual situation? Is the establishment of a subsidiary sufficient or does it need to be complemented by a transfer of the undertaking? The question arises whether the legality of a collective action prior to a relocation cannot be simply circumvented by the establishment of a subsidiary.

Maduro's use of coordinated action based on an *obligation* imposed on national unions is puzzling. The idea of a co-ordinated action seems to preclude a hierarchy between trade unions. It suggests that national unions co-ordinate their autonomous collective actions. In the case in question, the co-ordination was in the hands of a more centralized structure. This centralised structure did not impose obligations on its members like a public authority imposes obligations on citizens. The obligation stems from contractual freedom. The distinction is flawed.

184 See B. Bercusson, *Collective Action and economic freedoms before the European Court of Justice*, (ETUI, Brussels, 2007), pp. 40–45.

Other aspects of the proportionality test are identical to those applied in *Schmidberger*. The Court advanced in a very generic way that the collective action as a restriction needs to be suitable for securing the attainment of the objective and not go beyond what is necessary in order to attain it.[185] Since the Court refuted the existence of a justified aim for restricting the freedom to provide services in *Laval*, these aspects of the proportionality test have not been developed any further.

The Court seemed to suggest that the adequacy test needs to be assessed in a marginal way. It will be unlikely that a strike needs to be qualified as an inadequate means.[186] The Court did not examine the procedural issues of the proportionality test which lay at the heart of *Schmidberger*.[187] It was not disputed that the actions were in fact duly notified. Furthermore, it is difficult to see how the objective of the collective action could be attained in a different way.

These proportionality tests applied by the Court need to be distinguished from the proportionality test which has been introduced in the domestic regulations of some Member States. The latter proportionality test does not deal with the expressed goals of the collective actions. It deals with a relation between these expressed goals (revindications) and the effects (damage) of the collective action which is being contemplated or has been undertaken. *In casibus*, the exercise of both Avocates General and the Court is *not* about balancing the economic damage to the employer *vis-à-vis* the expressed goals of the trade unions organising a collective action. The exercise is about tackling a conflict between legal principles. The approach is much more qualitative in nature. The outcome of both opinions is illustrative in this regard. In *Laval* where the damage was much more harshly felt than in *Viking*, the analysis by Mengozzi amounts to a rather favourable assessment of the collective action. In *Viking* which was only confronted with a threat of collective action, Maduro's opinion is much less favourable.

6.7. THE *VIKING* JUDGEMENT INTRODUCES RESTRICTIONS ON THE RIGHT TO TAKE COLLECTIVE ACTION WHICH ARE INCOMPATIBLE WITH INTERNATIONAL LABOUR STANDARDS

The attitude of the Court implies that collective actions which are at odds with the freedom of establishment will be made subject to a substantial *proportionality*

185 See *Viking* judgement, §75; *Laval* judgement §101; *Viking* judgement, §75.

186 See *Viking* judgement, §86.

187 See in this respect: the Conclusions of the ECSR with regard to Belgium: Conclusions XVI-1, pp. 71–73.

test. In *Laval,* the adoption of such a test by the Court amounts to an assessment of what constitutes a just and fair level of remuneration. Thus, the Court introduced restrictions on the exercise of collective action which are at odds with the Conclusions of the *European Committee on Social Rights.* This Committee of independent experts supervises the European Social Charter. It has affirmed that the proportionality test is incompatible with Article 6, in conjunction with Article 31 of the European Social Charter insofar as it will urge judges to impede the autonomous assessment of the appropriate character of some demands by trade unions and workers. They should be autonomous in defining these interests and to assess whether it is appropriate to defend these interests through collective action.

It is noteworthy that the procedural *ultimum remedium* test that the Court applied in *Schmidberger* was rejected by the ECSR on identical grounds.[188]

7. *CURIA LUXEMBURGENSIS LOCUTA, SED CAUSA NON FINITA EST*

The judgements in *Laval* and *Viking* have set restrictions on the right to take collective action as protected on the domestic level which are unprecedented and which were scarcely conceivable until recently. The case law of the Court of Justice constitutes a challenge to trade unions, to domestic courts as well as to Member States willing to safeguard a fundamental workers' right which is often constitutionally anchored in their domestic legal order. The question arises whether the Court has indeed pronounced a final judgement on this issue and whether it will bring an end to the battle which has commenced. In our view, both judgements do provide scope for effective responses.

A comparative overview of *Schmidberger, Viking* and *Laval* gives rise to a great deal of legal insecurity regarding the precise role of the Court of Justice in dealing with conflicts between so-called fundamental freedoms and fundamental rights proper. In all three cases, the Court prescribes a proportionality test to deal with such a conflict. In *Schmidberger* and *Laval,* the Court tackled the conflict in favour and to the detriment of the fundamental rights concerned. The collective action at stake in *Laval* failed to meet a just and legitimate aim. A proportionality test is not just prescribed, but is actually applied. In *Viking,* the Court ordered the referring judge to tackle the conflict according to the rule of proportionality.

188 *Supra*: note 165. F. Dorssemont "De prullenbak een locus naturalis voor het leerstuk van misbruik van stakingsrecht? Over collectieve actie, syndicale autonomie en opportuniteits-controle", [2002] *Nederlands Tijdschrift voor Sociaal recht*, pp. 320–329.

Apparently, the Court had some difficulty in defining its role. This is all the more puzzling, since all judgements have been given as a result of preliminary references.

The attitude of the Court seems to warrant the conclusion that the Court is reluctant to apply the proportionality test. The Court gives the impression of applying the proportionality test in a marginal way. It seems to apply it when the restriction on fundamental freedoms is obviously proportionate (*Schmidberger*) or obviously disproportionate *(Laval)*. Insofar as the Court invites the judge on the merits to apply the proportionality test, domestic judges could be tempted to apply the proportionality test in a marginal way as well. In this respect, they should only feel compelled to prohibit collective actions in so far as they constitute manifestly disproportionate restrictions on the so-called fundamental freedoms.

In fact, the Court seemed to indicate that at least one aspect of the proportionality test (*adequacy*) needs to be cautiously assessed.

Article 307 TEC states that the "rights and obligations arising from agreements concluded before 1 January 1958 or, for acceding States, before the date of their accession, between one or more Member States on the one hand, and one or more third countries on the other, shall not be affected by the provisions of this Treaty". The Court indicated in *Lévy* and *Minne*[189] that it is up to domestic judges to assess whether a State is under such a conflicting obligation arising from agreements previously concluded. Insofar as the obligation to respect the fundamental right to take collective action can be considered to flow from ILO Convention No. 87 (1948), judges have a choice explicitly granted by the TEC to disregard fundamental freedoms.[190]

The reasoning of the Court in *Laval* was influenced by the legal niceties which are inherent to the state of the art of Swedish Law. The absence of statutory legislation providing for minimum wages as well as the absence of an *explicit* provision lifting the option offered by Article 3(8) PWD can easily be remedied by statutory intervention. In our view, the question of whether the system of collective bargaining allowing an extension *sui generis* through recourse to boycott actions is an adequate means to transpose Article 3 of the PWD presupposes a proper understanding of the Swedish system of industrial relations. It is not up to the Court of Justice to adequately describe the state of the art of the Swedish transposition. However, it will be up to the Swedish judges or to judges applying Swedish law to determine whether that system implies a *decision* by the Member States within the meaning of Article 3(8) PWD. In this regard, there is an interesting divergence between the presentation offered by the Court of Justice in

189 ECJ, C-158/91 (*Levy*), and ECJ, C-13/93 (*Minne*).
190 This reponse has been supported by R. Eklund, (2006), 207.

its judgement and that which is presented by the Commission in its submission as well as by Advocate General Mengozzi. The issue does not affect the assessment of the implementation. It touches upon the content of the transposition. The determination of that content is not a matter for the Court of Justice to determine.

In so far as the judgement in *Laval* has been influenced by the unfortunate way in which the *Lex Brittania* has been drafted, it is clear that a revision of that law could be sufficient to tackle the objections raised by the Court. Thus, it is conceivable to restrict the social peace obligations *inter partes,* irrespective of their nationality.

The ITF could rephrase the binding circular blacklisting foreign service providers seeking to reflag their ships under a flag of convenience by means of a recommendation. Along the same lines, trade unions calling for a boycott could rely on solidarity instead of organising a solidarity strike. *Last but not least,* the rejection of an unconditional horizontal effect might be an incentive for workers to have recourse to so-called spontaneous collective actions. The approach of the Court of Justice provides evidence of an organic view of strike action. In such an approach common to German and British law, industrial action is seen as an action undertaken by trade unions, whereas it is essentially an action undertaken by workers with the assistance of *their* trade unions. In fact, the question arises whether recourse to more spontaneous kinds of collective action could not be sufficient to undermine the restrictive horizontal effect of the freedom of establishment and the freedom to provide services. It is difficult to imagine how the exercise of a fundamental workers' right by workers can be qualified as the exercise of legal autonomy.

In so far as domestic judges will feel forced to apply the proportionality test in a way which violates legal standards enshrined in ILO Convention No. 87 and the European Social Charter, it is essential that trade unions file a collective complaint[191] before the Freedom of Association Committee and the European Committee on Social Rights or present their observations to national reports during the supervision procedure. In so far as the European Union would actually accede to the ECHR, a request could be filed against the European Union at the ECHR to examine whether the restrictions on the right to take collective action are indeed compatible with Article 11 §2 ECHR.

---

191 The United Kingdom has not ratified the Additional Protocol to the European Social Charter Providing for a System of Collective Complaints. Sweden has indeed ratified it.

From a constitutional point of view, the best way to guarantee a more balanced view on economic governance would have been to adopt a Treaty provision which would guarantee that primary and secondary EC Law could not be used to undermine the exercise of fundamental rights as granted by the domestic constitutional law of the Member States. Inspiration could be drawn from a clause in the *Monti* Regulation. The ETUC is currently advocating such a clause.

FLEXICURITY AND THE EUROPEAN GLOBALISATION ADJUSTMENT FUND: PROPAGANDA OR PANACEA?

Prof. dr. Marc De Vos

Ghent University Law School

1. INTRODUCTION AND PURPOSE

Against the backdrop of growing economic globalisation and the Lisbon Strategy of turning the European Union into one of its winners, labour market performance has increasingly become the focus of attention. It is indeed widely understood and accepted that both economic growth and employment creation can mutually benefit from a labour market that is able to follow and sustain the dynamics of the market economy. When these dynamics increase because of the many volatile engines of globalisation, and when the crucible of change is the European Union where many domestic labour markets are often based on regulatory frameworks from an industrial past, the need to address labour market organisation becomes overwhelming.[1]

It is of course always hard to distinguish correlation from causation when analysing the nexus between economic performance, employment creation, and labour market organisation. However, it can be said that in approaching this nexus, countries across the European Union have basically adopted two major reform strategies. One the one hand, several continental European countries with rigid employment rules have focussed on piecemeal reform that leaves the traditional employment protection largely unaffected while providing for more flexible employment formulas at its margin. On the other hand, Scandinavian countries and the Netherlands are seen to have moderately modernised employment rules across the board, but with the complement of so-called "active labour market policies" that are both generous and rigorous. This second approach

1 See, more extensively, M. De Vos, Arbeidsrecht in transitie, forthcoming; R. Rovelli and R. Bruno, *Labour Market Policies, Institutions and Employment Rates in the EU-27*, IZA Discussion Paper 3502, 2008.

to labour market regulation has become known as "flexicurity", since it purportedly seeks to combine labour market flexibility with individual security.[2]

The European Union itself has not stayed neutral in the policy debate surrounding labour market reform. In furtherance of the European Community's treaty title on "Employment", the European Employment Strategy (hereinafter: EES) has sought to guide the employment policies on Member State level. In the process, the emphasis has squarely been put on the "flexicurity" option.

This article does not offer a comprehensive analysis of the Flexicurity mantra. Such analyses can easily be found in the booming literature on the subject. Rather, my aim is to put the overall drive for Flexicurity into the broader context of the European Union's labour law and its relationship with globalisation. I first seek to establish how "flexicurity" has emerged as a new and common model for social policy under the aegis of the European Employment Strategy (section 2). This common model is contextualized as a specific European response to the labour market dimension of globalisation (section 3), with the theory of "active labour market policies" as its most visible exponent in labour regulation (section 4). I then offer critical perspectives on the European Globalisation Adjustment Fund, the European Union's pioneering model for addressing globalisation through flexicurity (sections 5-6).

2. THE EMERGENCE OF "FLEXICURITY" AS A EUROPEAN SOCIAL POLICY MODEL

2.1. THE MARKET DIMENSION OF EUROPEAN LABOUR LAW[3]

National labour law of course reflects national reality. National realities vary widely, also within the European Union (hereinafter: EU). Notwithstanding this intrinsic variety, the historical origins of labour law at Member State level are often closely related to the 19th century's industrial revolution and the "Social Question" generated by a rapidly expanding capitalist society and a marginalized proletariat. Against this backdrop national labour law was initially conceived as a balancing force, imposing upon a supposedly omnipotent employer/capitalist minimum labour standards for the benefit of supposedly powerless workers. Whether this interference was done through legislation or through institutionalized

2 L. Nunziata, *European Employment and the Flexicurity Option*, 21.
3 Throughout this article "labour law" refers to the law governing the employment contract, whether individual or collective.

collective bargaining with unions, the result was typically a restriction of a free and unfettered market operation in employment. Traditional labour rules on health, safety, redundancy, working time, wages, and the like, all share a common purpose and nature of restricting free competition and free individual negotiation in the labour market.

For the purpose of this article it is important to realize that the birth of EU labour law was not in market restriction, but rather in market creation. As is well known, the 1957 Treaty of Rome contained very few labour law provisions. Where it did, these provisions were essentially included to facilitate the creation of what would in time become the internal market. Free movement of workers was an economic freedom aimed at ensuring the free flow of human capital in the European market. The provision for equal pay between men and women was adopted, not as the fundamental social right it eventually became, but as an economic protection against the dumping of cheap German female labour on the French labour market.[4] In essence, EU labour law was introduced to develop a flourishing European market which – it was believed – would take care of improved labour conditions by itself, without additional interference.

EU labour law has of course moved on substantially since 1957. A body of EU directives now imposes some form of common standards that, whether for the national or for the transnational or European dimension of the labour market, restrict and regulate the market economy. But besides all this "market correcting" the component of "market making" remains. It implies that the EU's labour law tradition is not genetically antagonistic towards a free market economy but contains strands that are both supportive and corrective in nature. This is a useful reminder and helps to understand the intellectual mindset that today has brought the EU to embrace Flexicurity through the process of the European Employment Strategy.

2.2. THE BLEAK PRESENT AND FUTURE OF EU LABOUR LAW

The development of common EU labour law has been a challenge throughout the entire history of the European integration process. EU regulations on labour issues, which require specific and fixed provisions on harmonised standards, are scarce and even forbidden in the core area of social policy.[5] EU labour law

4 See E. Ellis, *EU anti-discrimination law*, Oxford, Oxford University Press, 2005.

5 Article 137 TEC only allows Member States to "adopt (…) by means of directives, minimum requirements for gradual implementation".

directives often require prolonged negotiations with stakeholders and mostly result in flexible framework texts with some degree of internal flexibility, not unlike ILO conventions. The difficulties in finding sufficient common ground for labour law directives with meaningful common standards in furtherance of the EU's "social policy", are essentially threefold.

First, there are profound differences in labour market policy between different Member States. These differences are further exacerbated by differences in national social security systems, which are often tied to labour market institutions. Indeed, notwithstanding the political rhetoric about a so-called "European social model", there are so many differences among national welfare state and labour market systems that the very notions of a "European model" or a "Social Europe" are dubious. Economists typically distinguish between four different groups of social policy models within the EU, all with different features and institutions:[6]

- *Nordic countries* (Denmark, Finland and Sweden, plus the Netherlands) feature the highest levels of social protection expenditures and universal welfare provision. There is extensive fiscal intervention in labour markets based on a variety of "active" policy instruments. Strong labour unions ensure highly compressed wage structures.
- *Anglo-Saxon countries* (Ireland and the United Kingdom) feature relatively large social assistance of the last resort. Cash transfers are primarily oriented to people in working age. Activation measures are important as well as schemes conditioning access to benefits to regular employment. On the labour market side, this model is characterized by a mixture of weak unions, comparatively wide and increasing wage dispersion and relatively high incidence of low-pay employment.
- *Continental countries* (Austria, Belgium, France, Germany and Luxembourg) rely extensively on insurance-based, non-employment benefits and old-age pensions. Unions remain strong as regulations extend the coverage of collective bargaining to non-union situations.
- *Mediterranean countries* (Greece, Italy, Portugal and Spain) concentrate their social spending on old-age pensions and allow for a high segmentation of entitlements and status. Their social welfare systems typically draw on employment protection and early retirement provisions to exempt segments of the working age population from participation in the labour market. The wage structure is covered by collective bargaining and is strongly compressed.

6 See A. Sapir, *Globalisation and the Reform of European Social Models.*

The division in four groups of social policy models does not reflect the full length of national differences or the varying degrees of reform and change in different countries over time. Models are static, countries never are. More tellingly, the above classification does not include the 10 new Member States that joined the EU as of May 2004, nor the additions since then. EU enlargement has not only complicated the picture of social policy models. It has also confronted the EU with diversity in *economic performance and development* between Member States, to a degree and of a size hitherto unknown. This is the second factor that compromises the development of common EU labour law. The combination of political and economic differences is powerful antidote to common labour law standards, especially in view of the majority rules that govern the institutional decision making process within the EU.

Finally, the EU project lacks the *democratic will and cohesion* to supersede the diversity of models and interests by a common political project. As has been argued elsewhere, the EU lacks a political identity and a European *demos* that could serve as the stepping stone for a common social policy.[7] In the same vein, the absence of a truly European labour movement explains why the European social partners, who are institutionally able to develop EU labour law independently through the European social dialogue, have so far only achieved minor results beyond the sectorial level.[8]

2.3. THE DEVELOPMENT OF THE EUROPEAN EMPLOYMENT STRATEGY (EES): EUROPEAN EMPLOYMENT POLICY AS AN ALTERNATIVE FOR EUROPEAN LABOUR LAW

The political en institutional incapacity to generate common EU labour law developed at a time when a growing consensus in academic and policy circles identified the labour market woes of many EU Member States as related to common institutional and regulatory labour market features. A body of academic research was picked up, first by the OECD and later by the EU Commission to "conceptualise" European unemployment as being the result of underlying causes in labour market organisation that were, in varying degrees, common to most of the troubled Member States.[9] In other words: the EU's potential to develop EU labour law defaulted at a time when it was increasingly considered as useful or even needed. This paradox fuelled a European drive in

7 See M. Büchs, *New Governance in European Social Policy*, 9–10.
8 M. De Vos, *De Europese CAO*, 11–32.
9 See D. Ashiagbor, *The European Employment Strategy*, 72 *et seq.*

the first part of the 1990s, helped by the necessary Green Paper and White Paper, towards a more conscious European *employment* policy, irrespective of the febrile state of the EU's social policy.

An Employment Title was ultimately inserted into the Treaty establishing the European Community (hereinafter: TEC) as part of the Amsterdam Treaty. The essence of the Employment Title, set out in Articles 125 to 130 TEC, is the development of a *"coordinated strategy for employment and particularly for promoting a skilled, trained and adaptable workforce and labour markets responsive to economic change"* (Article 125): the European Employment Strategy (EES). The coordination rests upon a broad framework of employment policy guidelines promulgated by the Union and designed for national implementation. The operations of the EES have been analyzed thoroughly elsewhere and can be summarised as follows:[10]

- The European Council adopts conclusions on the employment situation in the Union, on the basis of a joint annual report prepared by the Council and the Commission.
- These conclusions allow the Commission to propose employment policy guidelines that are eventually adopted by the Council and are now part of a three-yearly comprehensive set of guidelines.[11]
- The Member States shall take the employment guidelines into account in their employment policies (Article 128.2 TEC) and are obliged to report, in National Reform Programmes (known as National Action Plans for Employment till 2005), on the principal measures taken to implement the employment policy.
- The Council carries out an examination of the implementation of the employment policies and can make recommendations to Member States.
- The Council and the Commission make a joint annual report to the European Council on the employment situation in the Community and on the implementation of the guidelines for employment.

The launch and development of the EES signal some major shifts in the EU's strategy for labour market regulation. The EES represents a down-to-earth result oriented focus on employment, both in quantitative and in qualitative terms. This contrasts markedly with the more lofty social policy that essentially aims for social progress in working conditions. In essence the EES brings the EU's labour market approach closer to general economic development and policy, exemplifying again the historical interconnectedness of labour market policy and economic

10 See D. Ashiagbor, *The European Employment Strategy*, 127 *et seq.*

11 At the time of writing: Council Decision of 12 July 2005 on Guidelines for the employment policies of the Member States, (2005/600/EC).

policy at EU level. One can even assume a degree of subordination of the former to the latter, to the extent that the employment policies adopted by the Member States are legally required to be consistent with the EU's Broad Economic Policy Guidelines (Article 126.1 TEC). In the context of the Lisbon Strategy which is addressed hereunder, the employment guidelines are part of "Integrated Guidelines for Growth and Jobs", together with macro-economic and micro-economic guidelines. Labour market policy, in the shape of the EES, is again seen as an instrument for overall economic progress in the internal market, not unlike the Community's initial labour law provisions of 1957.

Only this time, we are indeed talking *policy* and not *law*, and that is a paradigm shift. Given the aforementioned difficulties in developing common labour market standards, the EES prefers an open method of coordination through guidelines over partial harmonisation through legislation. EU employment policy guidance is the substitute for EU employment law standards. In the process, the partially democratic adoption procedure of directives is lost for a bureaucratic procedure which often sees interference by stakeholders and Member States but attributes only an advisory role for the European Parliament. Moreover, experience has shown that national parliaments typically have often little to zero input in the national action plans. The result is a procedure that lacks transparency and that, notwithstanding many statements about participation, has serious legitimacy issues from a democratic perspective.[12] Ironically, the lack of *demos* that is partially responsible for the dearth of EU labour law has thus bread a strategy that further undermines the future and potential of any European *demos*.

2.4. FROM EES TO THE LISBON AGENDA AND TO FLEXICURITY

An early assessment of the EES predicted that it would be little more than a basis for the exchange of information, given the relative weakness of the coordinating role accorded to the central organs of the European Union.[13] This prediction was always hazardous, given that the open method of coordination has been proven effective in other EU areas even without any basis in the TEC.[14] It has been proven wrong with the arrival of the EU strategy, first adopted at the Lisbon European Council in March 2000, to make the EU by 2010 *"the most competitive and dynamic knowledge-based economy in the world capable of sustainable economic*

[12] See the extensive and incisive critique in M. Büchs, *New Governance in European Social Policy*, 130 *et seq.*

[13] C. Barnard and S. Deakin, *A year of living dangerously? EC social rights, employment policy, and EMU*, 356.

[14] See extensively M. Büchs, *New Governance in European Social Policy*, 97 *et seq.*

growth with more and better jobs and greater social cohesion". The EES has been subsumed within the overall Lisbon Strategy. In other words, the European Employment Strategy has become an instrument in achieving the Lisbon Strategy, once again emphasising the close link between employment and economic policy at EU level. As a result, the political capital of the EES has risen to the hype value of the Lisbon Strategy of which it is now an integral part.

Even though later European Councils surveyed the progress in the delivery of the Lisbon Strategy, the 2004 Kok Report "*Facing the challenge*" highlighted underperformance in many areas, including the labour market. The report recommended a balance between flexibility and security in order to increase the adaptability of workers and enterprises in an ever changing economy. Following its negative mid-term evaluation, the Lisbon Strategy was revamped to focus on delivering stronger, longer-lasting growth and more and better jobs. The Commission stepped up the debate on labour market reforms through its bold 2006 Green Paper "*Modernising labour law to meet the challenges of the 21st century*", which posed "a flexible and inclusive labour market" as a key challenge and advocated a "flexicurity" approach. This was followed in 2007 by the publication by the Commission of "*Towards Common Principles of Flexicurity: More and better jobs through flexibility and security*". This document capitalizes on the informal endorsement of "flexicurity" at the political level of the European Council in 2006 and provides both a general conceptual framework and concrete pathways to determine and develop agendas of flexicurity at Member State level.

For the European Commission, reflecting on a wide and recent body of research, flexicurity is defined as "an integrated strategy to enhance, at the same time, flexibility and security in the labour market". "Flexicurity is about striking the right balance between flexible job arrangements and secure transitions between jobs so that more and better jobs can be created. *Flexibility* is about developing flexible work organisations where people can combine their work and private responsibilities, where they can keep their training up-to-date and potentially have flexible working hours. It is also about giving both employers and employees a more flexible environment for changing jobs. *Security* means 'employment security' – to provide people with the training they need to keep their skills up-to-date and to develop their talent as well as providing them with adequate unemployment benefits if they were to lose their job for a period of time."[15]

It is worth quoting this passage in full because it both defines the essential tenants of the flexicurity mantra and marks its elevation to European Union orthodoxy.

---

15 European Commission, *Towards Common Principles of Flexicurity: More and better jobs through flexibility and security*, 2007.

It now remains to further define and apply the flexicurity concept. For this, the Commission offers concrete proposals and components for reforms at Member State level, stressing the need to address these as part of the overall machinery and purpose of the EES.

In barely a couple of years "flexicurity" has thus become a cornerstone of the EES which is itself tied to the inescapable Lisbon Strategy. Through the methodology of the EES not a single Member State can now afford to ignore a labour market philosophy that has become an article of faith in European policy. In the words of one of its most prolific scholars, flexicurity has now become the new paradigm for labour market policy reform in the EU.[16]

The advent of flexicurity as the *leitmotif* of EES is not surprising. Since the term was coined in the mid-1990s by a Dutch sociologist, "flexicurity" has quickly reached near cult status as the magic combination of seemingly conflicting necessities of labour market organisation: the flexibility required for companies in ever transitional economies and the security desired by workers. The former's flexibility used to go to the detriment of the latter's security, and vice-versa. A philosophy that is able to reconcile both is irresistible to a European Union in desperate need of a unifying model. *Philosophy* is indeed the right label. Flexicurity is not and cannot be a clearly defined regulatory model. It merely translates a broad win-win stance towards labour market regulation, suggesting the possibility of labour market reform beyond the traditional ideological divide. As such it is an easily marketable and defendable policy goal.

But when it comes down to determining its concrete implications, matters get much more complicated. It then becomes quickly apparent that the presentation of flexicurity as the osmosis of the formerly antagonists "flexibility" and "security" is really untrue. For the osmosis is only possible by embracing *a different type of security than previously attempted by most of the labour law*. The "security" advocated by flexicurity is of the dynamic type, seeking to obtain *general employment security in the labour market* by preparing, assisting and pushing individuals in and for the job transitions that follow from our flexible economy. Traditional labour law, on the other hand, has sought to realize security in a more static way by shielding the individual from transitions and thus protecting *specific job security at a particular employer.*

What flexicurity wants, therefore, is the partial dismantling of static labour law protection that counters flexibility, and its replacement with dynamic protection

16 T. Wilthagen, *Flexicurity: a new paradigm for labour market policy reform?*, WZB discussion paper 98–202, 1998.

that embraces flexibility but offers a new kind of security in return. This is particularly difficult towards the vested interests in static labour market protection, namely the 'insiders' of the labour market with relatively stable employment positions, and their unions. These vested interests know what they stand to lose but often remain to be convinced of the benefits. The flexibility part of flexicurity is indeed certain, whereas the security part is uncertain.

Moreover, to become effective in its quest for dynamic employment security, flexicurity requires labour law to focus more on the particular individual and its labour market position. Here too lies an obstacle, to the extent that the traditional labour law of the static kind is often also collective and standardized in its approach, with unions as the agents for a supposedly uniform and unison labour force. Flexicurity thus interferes with the traditional role model for unions, further complicating its reception at the level of Member States with powerful unions.

These implementation issues should not further detain us here. What is important to note, however, is that EU's embrace of "flexicurity" can be understood as yet another variation on the European theme of reconciling labour market regulation with the economic market, rather than opposing it. Flexicurity in many ways does not seek to limit or restrict the flexibility demanded by a market economy. Rather, it accepts this flexibility as economically necessary and beneficial. It merely seeks to offer personal forms of security for those involved in the otherwise flexible labour market. While national labour law is traditionally *market correcting*, and the original EU labour law was *market making*, the labour law translation of "flexicurity" can be called *market embracing*.

3. EU "FLEXICURITY" AND GLOBALISATION

As part of a Lisbon Strategy that aims to make the EU a paragon of international competitiveness, the European Flexicurity mantra has a clear political link with the furnace of global competition: globalisation. Understood in economic terms, globalisation marks the increased economic integration of markets and countries, driven forward by trade liberalisation, by the free flow of investment capital, by technological advances causing the "death of distance", and – to a lesser extent – by the liberalisation of labour migration. The current wave of economic globalisation – for indeed the phenomenon is far from new in human history – started roughly with the fall of the Berlin Wall in 1989. It may or may not have ended with the credit crisis of 2007–08 and with the subsequent great slump in the world economy; it is too soon to tell at this stage.

Even before the current global crisis, globalisation polarised both intellectuals and public opinion, especially in the western world where it not only meant new opportunities but also new competition. This is not the place to engage in this complex and often highly emotional debate. It is, however, important to realise that the European Union is a clear participant and therefore supporter of economic globalisation. Internationally the EU and its Member States are actively partaking in trade liberalisation through the World Trade Organisation. Internally, the EU is really a regional crucible of globalisation, since its essential mission is to realise an internal market among the ever growing number of Member States, built upon the "four freedoms" that are really *the* pillars of international economic integration: the free movement of goods, services, capital, and labour. Its entire "make-up" and identity make the European Union into one of the main agents of international economic integration.

The European Union therefore cannot be but supportive towards international economic integration. Indeed, the political challenge of "selling" globalisation to the national constituency is quite similar to that of "selling" European integration in the context of a European Union that has enlarged to integrate twelve developing countries from the Baltic and from Central and Eastern Europe.

The European Union has to have a story to convince public opinion of the benefits of free trade and international economic integration. The main tenant of that story is of course the acceptance, in line with the economic orthodoxies that have developed ever since David Ricardo discovered the law of comparative advantages, that free international trade is a win-win situation for all the countries involved. Within the EU, the internal globalisation of enlargement is equally presented as having boosted economic and employment growth in both old en new Member States alike.[17]

However, underneath the positive macro result of increasingly free trade lie micro trends with winners and losers. There are regions, sectors, companies, and individuals that benefit and there are equally regions, sectors, companies, and individuals that fail or benefit much less. In economic jargon these represent the *adjustment or transition costs* of an otherwise beneficial cycle of change, innovation, and growth. Transition costs are inherent in any economic progress and are minor compared to the overall gains of progress. It has been estimated – before the credit crisis kicked in – that the economic gains of globalisation outweigh its transition costs by a factor of between eight and ten to one. Even after internalising social and environmental implications, globalisation offers high

[17] See, inter alia, European Commission, *Enlargement, two years after: an economic evaluation*, 2006, 127 p. and *Five Years of an enlarged EU. Economic achievement and challengs*, 2009.

benefit/costs ratios. Moreover, free trade contributes to reducing global inequality and poverty.[18]

However limited they may or may not be, transition costs in lost jobs or market share are very obvious and concentrated. The gains in new jobs, new markets, new opportunities and lower prices on the other hand, are widely spread, less-easily attributed to trade reform, and are often mostly taken up by people other than those losing from the change. The media are easily mobilized by the easily identifiable losses of globalisation, whereas the large aggregate gains pass unnoticed. Against this backdrop, a small number of vested interests have leverage to lobby for their own protection while the public opinion is fed a distorted picture of the realities of globalisation. The fascination with the downside of globalisation, together with the increased speed, scale and international dimensions of globalisation, help to feed a climate of fear and distrust that transpires from opinion polls well before the current global crisis. Indeed, opinion polls in previous years have shown a growing disenchantment, with large majorities in western countries convinced that globalisation is bad for their country and with Stalinist majorities in favour of more government support for the victims of globalisation.[19]

Since free trade is essentially a political decision and since politicians want to get elected, the broad disenchantment with globalisation in the public opinion has generated a variety of policy responses. One obvious response is to maximize the number of winners and to make winners out of initial losers in a deliberate strategy of reform and innovation aimed at reaping the fruits of the new global opportunities. This, in essence, is the drift of the European Union's Lisbon Agenda. Tapping into globalisation's offerings, however, implies a willingness to change and make progress in a world of shifting balances where competitive threats and opportunities coexist. With a weary public opinion, such a positive and proactive response to globalisation becomes acceptable only if the transitional policies support those whose initial positions are threatened in the transition. It is here that "flexicurity" kicks in and becomes part of the European Union's response, both in political rhetoric and in policy, to globalisation.

Flexicurity, then, should be understood as a strategy, not just to promote the modernisation of labour regulation and improve labour market performance, but

18 See the extensive research summarised in K. Anderson and L. Alan Winters, *The Challenge of Reducing International Trade and Migration Barriers*, Copenhagen Consensus 2008.

19 See J. Morley and T. Ward, *Perceptions of globalisation: attitudes and responses in the EU*, Eurofound, 2008 and, inter alia, the surveys collected at www.worldpublicopinion.org and through the Eurobarometer at http://ec.europa.eu/public_opinion/.

also to sustain support for globalisation in the European Union. It is worth noting in that respect that workers in the Nordic countries, the fatherland of flexicurity, are much less likely to perceive globalisation as a threat than their counterparts in other European countries, even though their countries' economies are small and open.[20] The idea of security through change, rather than by limiting change, is not a dream after all.

Flexicurity is therefore part of the European Union's policy response to globalisation.[21] The whole philosophy of achieving security through change allows policy makers to embrace the otherwise beneficial changes that globalisation imposes. While offering 'security' to those affected by economic change, the engine of economic change itself can escape unscathed. The "market embracing" stance that lies behind Flexicurity thus extends beyond the EU to the wide thrust of globalisation. As part of the Lisbon Strategy, the aim of flexicurity is indeed to increase the European Union's performance in the global economy, while taking this global economy essentially for granted.

Nowhere is the link between globalisation and flexicurity clearer than in the creation of the European Globalisation Adjustment Fund (EGAF). As we shall see below, the EGAF was created by the European Union with the specific and symbolic purpose to use flexicurity as demonstrable globalisation relief.

4. FLEXICURITY AND ACTIVE LABOUR MARKET POLICIES (ALMP)

Flexicurity is seen to contain four essential components:[22]

- *Flexible and reliable contractual arrangements* (from the perspective of the employer and the employee, of "insiders" and "outsiders") through modern labour laws, collective agreements and work organisation;
- *Comprehensive lifelong learning (LLL)* strategies to ensure the continual adaptability and employability of workers, particularly the most vulnerable;
- *Effective active labour market policies (ALMP)* that help people cope with rapid change, reduce unemployment spells and ease transitions to new jobs;

---

20 *Ibid.*

21 See European Commission, *Towards Common Principles of Flexicurity: More and better jobs through flexibility and security*, 8.

22 European Commission, *Towards Common Principles of Flexicurity: More and better jobs through flexibility and security*, 2007.

- *Modern social security systems* that provide adequate income support, encourage employment and facilitate labour market mobility. This includes broad coverage of social protection provisions (unemployment benefits, pensions and healthcare) that help people combine work with private and family responsibilities such as childcare.

For the purpose of this article and its analysis of the European Globalisation Adjustment Fund (EGAF), our focus lies on active labour market policies (ALMP). To enable an assessment of the EGAF we must browse some general principles on the logic and effects of ALMP, drawing from the wide literature on the topic.[23]

The main role of ALMP is to promote employment by improving the match between offer and demand on the labour market. Matching offer and demand often requires a more individualised approach than general or group based employment programmes. As such the focus of ALMP is on "activating" – a rather harsh term for what is essentially a social objective – the targeted unemployed into matching employment. Its "active" approach distinguishes it from "passive" income measures that provide income stability that is not aimed at insertion or reinsertion into the labour market.

Underlying the drive towards ALMP is the understanding that such policies provide both better *efficiency* (*i.e.* better labour market performance) and more *equity* (*i.e.* support that is more targeted towards the needy) than the alternative. The assumption of better labour market performance overall is suggested by the macro-differences in labour market performance between roughly comparable countries or regions with different policies[24] and by the micro-level results of specific ALMP. However, irrefutable evidence of the positive impact on labour market performance would require an empirical comparison, under the same circumstances, of the actual outcomes for two comparable groups: one group with ALMP and a control group without ALMP. Such comparisons are almost always impossible to obtain, since ALMP are unlikely to experiment for academic purposes by slicing up the target group and discriminating between two comparable sections.

The *equity* strand of ALMP is closely related to the efficiency argument, in the sense that the overall efficiency of ALMP results from their effectiveness in being

---

23 See, inter alia, S. Carcillo and D. Grubb, *From Inactivity To Work: The Role Of Active Labour Market Policies*, OECD Social, Employment and Migration Working Papers No. 36, European Commission and RWI Essen, *Study on the effectiveness of ALMPs*, 2005; *OECD Employment Outlook 2005*, Chapter 4; G. Pierre, *A framework for active labour market policy evaluation*, ILO, 1999.

24 Comparing, for instance, the profiles and paths of the unemployed towards re-employment.

tailored towards the desired recipients of activation. As such, ALMP should avoid as much as possible the side effects that have typically plagued general employment measures, namely *deadweight loss* and *crowding out*. Deadweight loss roughly refers to the situation where an employment measure benefits a worker or job seeker (or his/her employer) who would have found similar gainful employment anyway. Crowding out roughly refers to the situation where an employment measure benefits a worker or job seeker at the expense of another candidate who does not benefit from the same support. Both efficiency and fairness suggest that ALMP should be targeted there where both these external effects are minimized. Indeed, the whole policy logic of the shift to ALMP in the Flexicurity mould is to abandon overbroad employment measures for closely targeted activation strategies.

An important caveat should, however, be added to this perspective. Some degree of *deadweight loss* and *crowding out* is intrinsic to all types of active employment policies. While efficiency and effectiveness are important policy considerations, one should not forget the *policy choice* that underlies all ALMP measures. Every ALMP by definition represents the political will to favour the labour market position of a particular group of beneficiaries. Whether this political will is effective and efficient *vis-à-vis* other groups and the labour market at large is not necessarily the only evaluation criterion. This is particularly relevant in assessing the European Globalisation Adjustment Fund, which indeed represents a political priority to single out and support those categories of workers that lose their jobs through the negative consequences of globalisation.

Moreover, two additional elements should be taken into account in the efficiency/effectiveness debate on ALMP. First, there will be an efficiency and effectiveness gain where the ALMP, notwithstanding its intrinsic potential of *deadweight loss* and *crowding out*, speeds up the matching process between offer and demand on the labour market. Time matters. Second, in assessing the impact of ALMP one should avoid the *lump of labour fallacy* that has misguided so many countries in adopting early retirement policies. There is no fixed amount of labour where the job of one person comes at the expense of another, or where the departure of a worker automatically opens a slot for a job seeker. On the contrary, employment generates more employment as it triggers more demand effects in the economy.[25]

While the preference of one category in an ALMP measure may therefore go to the detriment of another at the micro level of the firm, the macro effect on the labour market may still be positive for both. The micro effect is of course real and

---

25 This well known economic principle is now also recognised by the union researchers: G. Bosch and S. Schief, *Older employees in Europe between 'work line' and early retirement*, 590.

immediate for the people concerned, whereas the macro effect develops gradually and does not necessarily benefit the victims of the micro effect. At the end of the day, it is again the policy choice to target the labour market position of a particular group that has to decide on the trade-off. While such a policy choice is inevitable it also requires a deliberate reflection on costs and benefits, taking into account both efficiency and equity.

5. THE EUROPEAN GLOBALISATION ADJUSTMENT FUND: AN INTRODUCTION

5.1. ORIGIN AND MAIN PURPOSE

The intellectual and political origins of the European Globalisation Adjustment Fund (hereinafter: EGAF) lie across the Atlantic, in the United States. Ever since the Kennedy administration, the United States have had a federal programme of "*Trade Adjustment Assistance*" (TAA) aimed at offering assistance to eligible workers who are adversely affected by trade. Available assistance includes job training, Trade Readjustment Allowances, job search, relocation, and other services concerning re-employment. The economic necessity and effectiveness of TAA is heavily debated among researchers and its empirical support is patchy at best. But political support for the programme has never disappeared, as budget, scope and beneficiaries of trade adjustment assistance have consistently grown over the decades.[26]

In the European Union, a European programme for direct assistance to displaced workers was advocated in the influential 2003 Sapir Report "*An Agenda for a Growing Europe*". The report's authors saw the displacement assistance as an attractive European complement to national employment policies. They had no qualms in recognising the essentially political purpose of their proposal: "To the extent that EU policies contribute to increasing job security, they could also contribute to alleviating the pain generated, *inter alia,* by wider and deeper EU integration."[27] In other words: European trade adjustment assistance from its very inception was conceived as a measure to help the public opinion swallow the downsides of international and European economic integration. Its primary

---

26 For critical assessments, see D. Froning, *Trade Adjustment Assistance: A Flawed Program*, The Heritage Foundation, 2001; S. James, *Maladjusted. The Misguided Policy of Trade Adjustment Assistance*, Cato, 2007; D. Markheim and J. Sherk, *Trade Adjustment Assistance: Getting Reform Right*, The Heritage Foundation, WebMemo 1682, 2007; H.F. Rosen, *Strengthening Trade Adjustment Assistance*, Peterson Institute, PB08-2, 2008.

27 A. Sapir et al., *An Agenda For a Growing Europe Making the EU Economic System Deliver,* 2003.

economic rationale was not the labour market reintegration of displaced workers as such, but the overall openness to international trade and to European integration. This understanding is crucial for evaluating the relevance or irrelevance of what eventually became the EGAF.

Commission President Barroso proposed the creation of a European Globalisation Fund in a letter on October 2005 before the Hampton Court Summit. It was stated that this fund would provide a European response to those adjusting to the consequences of globalisation, acting as a sign of solidarity from those who benefit from open trade to those who face the sudden shock of losing their job. The proposal was endorsed at the December 2005 European Council, where there was general agreement among European leaders on the need to address the adverse effects of changing trade patterns on workers. The EGAF was passed by Council Regulation 1927/2006 on 20 December 2006 (hereinafter: the EGAF Regulation), and the fund is operational since 1 January 2007.

The EGAF symbolizes first and foremost the European Union's desire to show that it is doing its part in addressing the negative consequences of globalisation. Of course, as we have seen, the European Union's response is not and cannot be a repudiation of globalisation as such. On the contrary, the preamble to the EGAF Regulation emphasises the Union's support for external trade and underscores that a long-term and sustainable European strategy for trade policy is the fundamental answer to the drawbacks of globalisation. It can therefore be safely stated that the EGAF is an exercise to symbolically provide for globalisation relief so as to make globalisation more sellable to a public opinion which is increasingly concerned with its impact. As such the EGAF is not only there to help the victims of globalisation but also globalisation itself.

Secondly, and equally symbolic, the relief provided to the victims deliberately wants to be dynamic and active, aimed at the reinsertion of these victims into the labour market through active labour market policies. The EGAF is designed to help fund a flexicurity policy for generating employment security for the affected workers who lost their job because of globalisation. The EGAF therefore allows the EU to lead by example in its own Flexicurity agenda. In short, the EGAF is an emblematic reminder of the nexus between Flexicurity and globalisation.

The remainder of this section will briefly explore the legal construction of the EGAF. The subsequent section offers critical perspectives that demonstrate both the limits and the drawbacks of this symbolic standard bearer of Flexicurity.

5.2. SCOPE AND TARGET GROUP

"With the aim of stimulating economic growth and creating more jobs in the European Union", the EGAF is established "to enable the European Union to provide support for workers made redundant as a result of major structural changes in world trade patterns due to globalisation where these redundancies have a significant adverse impact on the regional or local economy" (Article 1.1 EGAF Regulation).

The Commission's official "Guidance for submission of applications" (hereinafter: the Guidance[28]) requires applicants to provide a reasoned analysis of the link between the planned or actual redundancies and the major structural changes in world trade patterns. Relevant statistics and data, at the most appropriate geographical and sectoral level, should be provided to support the contention that the redundancies are connected to major structural changes in world trade patterns due to globalisation. In particular, clear evidence needs to be provided to demonstrate that the redundancies follow factors such as a substantial increase of imports into the EU, a rapid decline of the EU world market share in a given sector, or a delocalisation to third countries.

A financial contribution from the EGAF shall be provided where major structural changes in world trade patterns lead to a serious economic disruption, notably a substantial increase of imports into the European Union, or a rapid decline of the EU market share in a given sector or a delocalisation to third countries, which results in a minimum number of redundancies over a certain reference period. The number and the period differ with the level at which the impact is assessed (Article 2 EGAF Regulation):

(a) At least 1 000 redundancies over a period of 4 months in an enterprise in a Member State, including workers made redundant in its suppliers or downstream producers.
(b) At least 1 000 redundancies, over a period of 9 months, particularly in small or medium-sized enterprises, in a NACE 2 sector in one region or two contiguous regions at NUTS II level.
(c) In small labour markets or in exceptional circumstances, an application may be considered admissible even if these conditions are not entirely met, when redundancies have a serious impact on employment and the local economy.

It should be noted that the cited intervention criteria refer to "world trade patterns" as opposed to European trade patterns, implying that shifts in intra-European

28 Consulted on the internet in January 2009.

trade patterns can never lead to the intervention of the EGAF. This interpretation is corroborated by the exclusive reference to "imports into the EU" and "decline of EU market share", both of which again point to trade patterns between the EU and the rest of the world. The exclusion of European trade patterns is remarkable, since the European Union's own economic integration, especially in the wake of the recent enlargements, can indeed be seen as part of globalisation and as a form of internal globalisation.

The Guidance specifies a number of the intervention criteria, notably for the identification and the calculus of dismissals in relationship to reference period. Dismissals are understood to hinge on notification of dismissal, covering all workers who have been notified by their employer of his/her intention to terminate the employment contract.

The Guidance also elabourates quite extensively on the need for the applicant to break down and describe the categories of workers affected by the redundancies. This should allow for a more careful assessment of the actual cause of the redundancies for which an intervention is sought.

Guidance is clearly needed for the open ended exception of "small labour markets" or "exceptional circumstances", with a "serious impact on employment and the local economy". However, the reader finds little more than the confirmation that the applicant should justify its interpretation of the event as falling under this exception. This obviously leaves room for flexibility but also for quite uncomfortable discretion.

5.3. ELIGIBLE ACTIONS

The EGAF is designed to co-fund *active labour market measures* that form part of a coordinated package of personalised services designed to re-integrate redundant workers into the labour market, including (Article 3 EGAF Regulation):

(a) for job-search assistance, occupational guidance, tailor-made training and re-training, including information and communication technology skills and certification of acquired experience, as well as for outplacement assistance and entrepreneurship promotion or aid for self-employment;
(b) for special time-limited measures, such as job-search allowances, mobility allowances or allowances to individuals participating in lifelong learning and training activities; and
(c) for measures to stimulate in particular disadvantaged or older workers, to remain in or return to the labour market.

It is abundantly clear that the EGAF cannot finance passive social protection measures in the shape of mere income support. It is also clear that the EGAF Regulation lists the cited ALMP as mere examples. Other types can therefore also be proposed for funding. Besides that, there is very little in the EGAF Regulation to steer the process, apart from the self-evident confirmation that non-discrimination should permeate the process (Article 7). A lot is therefore apparently left to the Commission in deciding applications. The Guidance understandably goes to great lengths in requesting applicant countries to specify the target groups, the proposed personal services and their costs. But it does not offer any indication regarding the desired type, efficiency or effectiveness of the proposed ALMP. Indeed, as we shall see below, it is hard to determine to what extent the Commission actually has legal authority to question the discretionary choices in ALMP made by the applicant Member States.

An important report by the European Foundation for the Improvement of Living and Working Conditions has not hesitated in offering advice on the type of ALMP the EGAF should and should not sponsor, apparently assuming discretionary power as a matter of course. Since displacement is the focus, it is argued that the type of measures should be somewhat different than ALMP measures against unemployment in general.[29] For this author, no such a priori attitude seems necessary. What matters is that the services are "personalized" and therefore able to generate effect in the particular case, irrespective of the cause of unemployment.

Similarly, the report warns strongly against the EGAF supporting *temporary wage subsidies* for displaced workers, citing heavy deadweight loss and crowding out as the subsidized workers may find work regardless of the subsidy. In that case, it is argued, wage subsidies work as employer subsidies and are unfair towards other job seekers. This is a good illustration of the efficiency and equity debate surrounding ALMP measures, as outlined above. However, it fails to take into consideration some elements of the equation: the political will to promote the employment of the particular group of workers displaced through globalisation, the time gains when supported workers find new jobs sooner than without ALMP, and the beneficial impact of their employment for the economy and the labour market as a whole. These elements nuance the picture substantially and may tilt the balance in favour of temporary wage subsidies, especially since these have shown robust employment results at micro level. In other words: the combination of political priority, rapid results and overall benefits may justify the support of temporary wage subsidies notwithstanding their intrinsic limitations.

[29] European Foundation for the Improvement of Living and Working Conditions, *European Restructuring Monitor Report 2007, Restructuring and employment in the EU: The impact of globalisation*, 63.

In any event, from a legal perspective, the EGAF Regulation does not exclude or restrict any type of ALMP as long as it matches the broad categorisation cited above.

5.4. PROCEDURE

The Member States and the Commission drive the procedure. It is up to the Member State, not to any globalisation stricken employer, worker or union, to submit the application for EGAF intervention with all the information as required by the EGAF Regulation (Article. 5) and the Guidance developed by the European Commission.

The Commission itself "evaluates and proposes as quickly as possible, the amount of financial contribution, if any, that may be made within the limits of the resources available" (Article 10 EGAF Regulation). The actual decision on an application is taken by the European Parliament upon the proposal of the European Commission (Article 12 EGAF Regulation). When making its assessment:

- the Commission shall assess, in consultation with those Member State(s), whether the conditions for making a financial contribution under this Regulation are met (Article 5.5);
- the Commission shall particularly take into account the number of workers to be supported, the proposed actions and the estimated costs (Article 10.1).

It is therefore clear that the Commission must verify whether the formal conditions for making financial contribution are met and that it therefore has some discretionary power in interpreting these conditions. However, it is unclear to what extent the Commission can make value judgments regarding the choice of protected workers or the choice of active labour market policies, especially in situations where enough financial resources are available. This is an important issue as applications organised by Member States are likely to reflect their policy choices and priorities. Does the Commission have the legal authority, beyond the marginal case of avoidance of abuse and patent failure, to advise on applications on its assessment of their intrinsic merits alone?[30]

[30] For this and for other questions regarding the functioning of the EGAF; see: M. De Vos, *European Globalisation Adjustment Fund. The Law and Policy of Trade Adjustment Assistance in the European Union*, forthcoming.

6. THE EUROPEAN GLOBALISATION ADJUSTMENT FUND: A CRITIQUE

6.1. A PROBLEMATIC SCOPE

As we have seen, the EGAF is there *"to provide support for workers made redundant as a result of major structural changes in world trade patterns due to globalisation where these redundancies have a significant adverse impact on the regional or local economy"* (Article 1.1 EGAF Regulation). The use of EGAF resources is therefore dependent on no less than *five cumulative conditions* that all require fulfilment:

- The redundancies should be the *result* of major structural changes in world trade patterns due to globalisation, i.e. should be *caused* by such changes.
- The required cause of the redundancies is a change in "world trade patterns", as opposed to *mere European or regional trade patterns.*
- The required change in world trade patterns should be *structural*, as opposed to *cyclical.*
- The required structural change in world trade patterns should be a "major" one, as opposed to *minor or average*. The preamble of the EGAF Regulation refers to "the shock of serious economic disruption".
- The required major structural change in world trade patterns should be due to *"globalisation".*

Given the fluidity and elusiveness of the term "globalisation", it is quite startling to find the concept without any clarification whatsoever in the EGAF Regulation. The connection to world trade patterns implies, one supposes, a focus on shifts in international trade. The Commission, in its Guidance with application instructions to the Member States, mentions "factors such as a substantial increase of imports into the EU, a rapid decline of the EU world market share in a given sector, or a delocalisation to third countries." This is illustrative, but it remains unclear as to what underlying currents of such trade shifts actually classify as "globalisation" for the sake of the EGAF.

And this is only the beginning. Assuming that a shift in trade patterns qualifies as "globalisation", it can only authorize EGAF intervention if it is the *cause* of the redundancies for which an active labour market response is desired. The combined expertise of economists in the world has difficulty establishing whether job displacements are actually caused by trade effects. Indeed, the establishment of such a causal relation is essentially impossible, since there will always be several factors that interplay in causing redundancies, especially in the context of international trade. The plain fact that similar companies in similar markets can perform differently in the face of international competition proves that the impact of globalisation is in part always dependent on the managerial and entrepreneurial reaction to it. It is therefore clear that the causal link with globalisation, upon which the intervention of the EGAF depends, is intrinsically unfathomable and intrinsically prone to reward failed companies and failed policies. By helping displaced workers the EGAF risks also paying for bad policy and bad management. As we shall see, this risk for externalisation of policy and management costs is further compounded by the partly political procedure that drives the EGAF's application process.

Whereas both globalisation and its causal link to redundancies are open and manipulable concepts, the EGAF further requires distinguishing between cycles and structures, and between major or other changes in world trade patterns. Is there really anyone who seriously believes that the realisation of these cumulative conditions can be established objectively? Only the minimum number of redundancies has been set by the EGAF Regulation, but even then there is room for discretionary choices in "small labour markets or in exceptional circumstances". It really beggars belief to find the preamble to the EGAF Regulation boldly declaring that: *"Actions under this Regulation should be defined according to strict intervention criteria relating to the scale of economic dislocation and its impact on a given sector or geographical area (...)"*.

The scope of the EGAF Regulation is simply unbearably vague and therefore leaves too much room for discretionary policy choice. Given the partly political nature of any application process driven forward by Member States, this is truly problematic. At the least a transparent and public set of parameters interpreting and applying the conditions of the EGAF Regulation would be desirable. This is not currently available, notwithstanding the Commission's best efforts to offer extensive guidance for the application process.

The Commission has indeed made a valuable effort in streamlining the application process to the EGAF through a standard set of instructions.[31] The applicant Member State is asked to provide a reasoned analysis of the link between the planned or actual redundancies and the major structural changes in world trade patterns. Relevant statistics and data, at the most appropriate geographical and sectorial level, should be provided to support the contention that the redundancies are connected to major structural changes in world trade patterns due to globalisation. In particular, clear evidence needs to be provided to demonstrate that the redundancies follow factors such as a substantial increase of imports into

31 Application for a contribution from the European Globalisation adjustment Fund (EGAF), available at http://ec.europa.eu/employment_social/EGAF/keydocs_en.html.

the EU, a rapid decline of the EU world market share in a given sector, or a delocalisation to third countries. Data related to delocalisation to third countries should demonstrate there is a substitution of production previously carried out within the EU by production in a third country.

These instructions contain useful guidance for the analysis of the cumulative conditions discussed above. However, they do not as such clarify how the Commission interprets these conditions concretely. Such an interpretation is urgently needed to counter the unbearable lightness of the EGAF Regulation's scope.

6.2. A PROBLEMATIC TARGET GROUP

While ALMP measures are no zero sum game, they inherently imply a degree of trade-off between the interests of the targeted and promoted group on the one hand, and the general mass of unemployed or job seekers on the other hand. As we have seen, policy makers should therefore carefully consider efficiency and equity when taking the political decision to promote the labour market position of a particular group through ALMP.

It should be stressed here that the number of workers who lose their jobs through the effects of globalisation are but a small percentage of the enormous overall churn in economies and labour markets characterized by a continuous process of job creation and job destruction.[32] What is the rationale and justification for targeting scarce taxpayer money towards that rare and elusive bread of workers who are displaced due to globalisation? This question is particularly relevant since *even the perspective of the displaced worker himself* does not warrant a specific focus on displacement trough globalisation. Indeed, as a leading scholar in the field has remarked:

> *"For most displaced workers, what matters is the kind of job lost and the kind of job regained. Why the job was lost does not matter much at all. If workers and consequences are alike, across differing causes of job loss such as increasing foreign competition, technological change, downsizing, then policymakers should consider adjustment policy for all displaced workers, and broaden eligibility beyond 'trade-displaced workers'."*[33]

---

32 On job creation and destruction, see S. Davis, J. Haltiwanger en S. Schuh, *Job creation and destruction*, The MIT Press, Cambridge, 1996.

33 L. Kletzer, *Job loss from imports: Measuring the Loss*, 6.

Let us begin by recognising the differences in labour market position between displaced workers and the unemployed in general. Having lost their previous occupation, displaced workers suffer what is known as a loss of firm specific capital[34]:

- A job may be the outcome of a long process of searching for and trying out various jobs before finding one that matches the worker's competencies and personal preferences. Thus when this job is lost it may require another lengthy matching process. This may be particularly problematic for older workers.
- The competencies of the displaced workers may be linked to the lost job and be specific to that place of work, i.e. contain much firm-specific human capital which is not marketable on the external labour market. This firm-specific capital may be acquired by on-the-job training or experience at the workplace and so is likely to be strongly correlated with the length of service at the firm.
- Employees with long service may have accrued seniority rights that will be lost upon losing the job. These include job security rights and seniority wages.
- The loss of a job can be a very stressful event both in financial and social terms. This is a problem itself and may impact negatively on the chances of getting a new job, particularly for older workers with long seniority.

Since displaced workers are objectively distinguishable from the generally unemployed, there is little risk of their favourable treatment through targeted ALMP running into discrimination claims. However, this legal justification is only the beginning. ALMP are labour market policies in favour of a particular group and it is from that labour market angle that their justification should primarily be considered.

One argument in favour of a European policy for displaced workers is that it fills a gap. National active labour market policy is often aimed at combating unemployment in general. Few national measures are specifically designed for displaced workers and fewer still for those who are displaced because of the negative side of globalisation. Since the EU itself, through its internal and external free trade policies, is an active agent in the globalisation game it would make sense to have a European answer to the transition costs of free trade for identifiable workers.[35] This argument is tantamount to justifying regulation for the sake of regulation. It does not address the economic or labour market rationale for

34 European Foundation for the Improvement of Living and Working Conditions, *European Restructuring Monitor Report 2007, Restructuring and employment in the EU: The impact of globalisation*, 74.

35 European Foundation for the Improvement of Living and Working Conditions, *European Restructuring Monitor Report 2007, Restructuring and employment in the EU: The impact of globalisation*, 63.

targeting displaced workers in ALMP regulation. Precisely that rationale is one of the key weaknesses of a policy that, like the EGAF, channels assistance towards job displacement through international competition.

Research in the US has indeed shown that the economic costs of job loss do not vary significantly by sector, specifically when comparing those sectors that are subject to foreign competition and those that are not. The economic costs of job loss vary mostly by individual characteristics and local labour market conditions. The economic cause of unemployment is of limited relevance for the subsequent labour market performance of the unemployed.[36] There is thus little substantive reason to target assistance to globalisation related job losses. Displaced workers do sustain subsequent economic loss in labour market outcome but that loss is mostly short term and related to the macroeconomic environment underlying their displacement.[37] From these perspectives at least, the case for targeting displaced workers looks weak at best.

The key difference in the circumstances of displaced workers and the unemployed in general is, of course, that the soon-to-be displaced workers currently hold a job. The period of notice, formal or otherwise, before the actual job loss may offer a useful window of opportunity for the implementation of ALMP measures. However, the fact that the intended beneficiaries are persons who were already employed before their actual or impending redundancy suggests an intrinsic labour market potential that many unemployed may not have. Why favour a group whose labour market position is better than many of the unemployed? The probability of the EGAF engendering a *deadweight loss* of funding towards workers that would find work anyway is arguably greater than with measures aimed at the unemployed. How fair is the EGAF, given the massive needs of the otherwise unemployed?

The issue of fairness and efficiency is further exacerbated by the dependence, as a rule, of EGAF intervention on massive redundancies of at least 1000 employees. The crowding-out effect of ALMP measurers as discussed above – i.e. their selection of the beneficiary at the expense of another job seeker – is more significant when there are a large number of other job seekers in the local labour force. Consequently, if the restructuring case is large relative to the local labour market – as will often be the case with the requirements for EGAF intervention – the risk

36 European Foundation for the Improvement of Living and Working Conditions, *European Restructuring Monitor Report 2007, Restructuring and employment in the EU: The impact of globalisation*, 82.

37 European Foundation for the Improvement of Living and Working Conditions, *European Restructuring Monitor Report 2007, Restructuring and employment in the EU: The impact of globalisation*, 72–73; see L. Kletzer, *Job loss from imports: Measuring the Loss.*

of crowding-out will become more problematic. EGAF intervention therefore runs the risk of promoting the re-employment of displaced workers with a negative impact on the short term job prospects of weaker groups in unemployment, such as the young, the elder or the immigrants.

In a cynical confirmation of old fortunes, globalisation adjustment may thus continue to entrench the favourable position of the *insiders* on the labour market, while further reducing the changes of labour market entry for the *outsiders*. This cannot and should not be the goal of the EGAF. There is a crucial need for complementary reform at Member State level, to stimulate more job creation in general, to optimize job intakes on the labour market and to develop general activation in unemployment insurance. Without such reforms, which are much more profound and structural than globalisation adjustment, the latter's intrinsic trade-off between the displaced workers and other job seekers becomes socially untenable.

The economic case for targeting workers displaced through globalisation is thus weak while the risk of perverse effects is strong. The main rationale for the EGAF is therefore clearly political. The EGAF is a political showcase to illustrate the EU's social agenda in the face of globalisation. It addresses the public opinion's perceptions about globalisation in the hope of ensuring their support for a process that has widely benefited European economies and societies as a whole. As was stressed above, the gains from globalisation benefit the economies and societies as a whole. They remain often unseen or unappreciated by the individual or the general public. The losses from globalisation on the other hand are specific, identifiable and easily highlighted in the media. The limited and specific losses, rather than the important and general gains, tend to monopolize the attention. Displaced workers and their unions are a loud and visible minority. In this context, the EU has resorted to an action that is, at least from an overall economic and labour market perspective, essentially symbolic in nature while potentially pernicious in its effects.

6.3. A PROBLEMATIC PROCEDURE

The unbearably open ended scope and the questionable substantive merits of the EGAF programme, in terms of economic logic, labour market efficiency and equity, render its procedure crucially important. A programme which is essentially political in nature runs the risk of being steered politically. This is especially true since, as we have seen, the required causal relationship between globalisation and worker displacement is excessively hard to establish objectively.

Given this background, it is not particularly comforting to find the Member States in the driver seat for the submission of cases to the EGAF. There is a systemic risk of cherry picking and political gerrymandering if the EGAF's assistance can only be obtained through Member State intervention. This risk goes beyond the plain fact, emphasised above, that the EGAF risks becoming a tool to pay for failed policies at Member State level. The decision to submit or not to submit an application to the EGAF will always contain an element of national political choice, depending on the time and circumstances of the case. It is something the EGAF could really do without. One only has to look at the list of applications publicly reported by the EGAF to realize that they typically involve large showcases with big name companies, often national champions. This is an uncomfortable feeling for the EU citizen who is supposed to see the EU act to support the weak, rather than the strong, in the struggle of globalisation. Finally, when Member States write applications there is an increased likelihood that the proposed ALMP will translate the political favour of the moment, maybe even the preferred partner – public or private – of the moment. Transparency, efficiency, legitimacy, equity, and the market for employment services: all would be better served and better seen to be served by a more decentralized process involving the workers or their companies directly.

There is one final argument against the member state monopoly in submitting applications: speed. There is a strong case for starting the ALMP for displaced workers *as soon as possible*, even prior to the actual displacement process. The period of notice, formal or otherwise, before the effective job loss offers an important window of opportunity to avoid or anticipate the impending loss of labour market capacity that follows from redundancy. As we have seen, displaced workers indeed suffer from a loss of "firm specific capital" that reduces their status on the labour market. Effective ALMP will seek to address this decline rapidly while at the same time preferring a high-quality solution with long-term benefits to a quick fix with long term risks. This is particularly true for workers with long tenure at the firm, as a recent report from the European Restructuring Monitor has emphasised. For these workers, "the importance of an early start to job search may not be obvious and their lack of recent experience of external job search suggests that assistance may be necessary. Thus all involved parties (the appropriate public administrations, the social partners and the workers themselves) should grasp the window of opportunity that the notice period offers. In order for this to function properly it is vital that clear and early information on the impending job loss is provided."[38]

---

[38] European Foundation for the Improvement of Living and Working Conditions, *European Restructuring Monitor Report 2007, Restructuring and employment in the EU: The impact of globalisation*, 75.

Whereas speed is essential, it seems clear that the intervention of a national government and the necessary application procedure at EGAF level are likely to slow things down. A national government will have difficulty to intervene formally before the contours of a restructuring are clear, i.e. after the internal information, consultation, and negotiation procedures have been exhausted. This delay now runs the risk of being further extended through the necessity of a separate application and approval procedure before the EGAF. If the EGAF money is to be spent effectively, its application process must be able to bear fruition on ALMP applicable during the window of opportunity offered by the notice periods of the affected workers. This should be a priority for the EGAF's administration. It may require such measures as urgency procedures, upstream application during the consultation phase at the company and prior to actual dismissal, or upfront payment by the Member State during or prior to the application process at the EGAF.

7. CONCLUSION: PROPAGANDA OR PANACEA?

Are Flexicurity and the EGAF about propaganda or about genuine labour market improvement? The fairest answer is that they are both. There is no doubting the European Union's seriousness of commitment to Flexicurity. Indeed, the Treaty establishing the European Community itself elevates the main tenets of Flexicurity to a constitutional principle: it commits both the EU and the Member States to "developing a coordinated strategy for employment and particularly for *promoting a skilled, trained and adaptable workforce and labour markets responsive to economic change*".[39] Where else do you see a particular labour market policy orientation enshrined as quasi-constitutional principle?

The choice for Flexicurity also ties in neatly with the unique European blend of labour market regulation, seeking to provide social protection while not repudiating but embracing the market economy. It offers a nice brand and a win-win approach to an otherwise dull and technocratic European Employment Strategy.

However, there can be little doubt as to the fundamental purpose of Flexicurity: it is first and foremost about sustaining, supporting and adapting to globalisation. Flexicurity is not just there to provide dynamic employment security for the victims of globalisation, it is also there to help globalisation itself. That is the perspective one should bear in mind when evaluating the European Globalisation

39 Article 125 TEC (my italics).

Adjustment Fund. On its own merits, the EGAF is truly an example of how *not* to have active labour market policies. Its scope is unbearably vague, its economic rationale highly questionable, its labour market effectiveness truly problematic, and its societal legitimacy patently contestable. Indeed, it is quite possible – as we have seen – that globalisation adjustment will actually continue to entrench the favourable position of labour market insiders at the expense of the existing outsiders. But that is really a side show. The EGAF is primarily a marketing tool to sustain support for globalisation by a sceptical and even hostile public opinion. If it succeeds in that purpose, then its rationale and justification are truly overwhelming given the massive and crucial importance of globalisation for the future prosperity in the entire European Union.

But the big picture alone cannot be the sole consideration. We cannot play games with displaced workers or with the general mass of unemployed. For their sake, and for the sake of labour market performance and social justice, the many fundamental problems with globalisation adjustment should be addressed. At the level of the European Union this will require a more rigorous and transparent framework and practice. At the level of the Member State it will require systemic development of ALMP so as to offer across the labour market what the EGAF supports for workers displaced by globalisation. This brings the story full circle to the European Employment Strategy, to Flexicurity and to its national implementation. Only in combination with a general and effective EES can the EGAF become acceptable labour market policy.

8. BIBLIOGRAPHY

K. Anderson and L. Alan Winters, *The Challenge of Reducing International Trade and Migration Barriers*, Copenhagen Consensus 2008, 72 pp.

D. Ashiagbor, *The European Employment Strategy*, Oxford University Press, 2005, 351 pp.

C. Barnard and S. Deakin, "A year of living dangerously? EC social rights, employment policy, and EMU", 1999 *Industrial Relations Journal: European Annual Review 1998*, pp. 355–372.

G. Bosch and S. Schief, "Older employees in Europe between 'work line' and early retirement", 13 *Transfer* 2007, pp. 575–593.

M. Büchs, *New Governance in European Social Policy*, New York, Palgrave, 2007, 206 pp.

S. Carcillo and D. Grubb, *From Inactivity To Work: The Role Of Active Labour Market Policies*, OECD Social, Employment and Migration Working Papers No. 36, 2006, 73 pp.

M. De Vos, "Arbeidsrecht in transitie", in *Liber amicorum Hubert Bocken*, Bruges, die Keure, 2009.

M. De Vos, "De Europese CAO", *Sociaalrechtelijke Kronieken*, dossier 2002, pp. 11–32.

European Commission, *Towards Common Principles of Flexicurity: More and better jobs through flexibility and security*, 2007, 38 pp.

European Commission and RWI Essen, *Study on the effectiveness of ALMPs*, 2005, 253 pp.

European Foundation for the Improvement of Living and Working Conditions (Eurofound), *European Restructuring Monitor Report 2007, Restructuring and employment in the EU: The impact of globalisation*, 2007, 106 pp.

L. Kletzer, *Job loss from imports: Measuring the Loss*, Washington, DC, Peterson Institute for International Economics, 2001, 144 pp.

J. Morley and T. Ward, *Perceptions of globalisation: attitudes and responses in the EU*, Eurofound, 2008, 37 pp.

L. Nunziata, *European Employment and the Flexicurity Option*, CESifo DICE Report, 4/2008, pp. 21–28.

G. Pierre, *A framework for active labour market policy evaluation*, ILO, 1999, 42 p.

A. Sapir, *Globalisation and the Reform of European Social Models*, Brussels, Bruegel, 2005, 19 pp.

PART II
DISCUSSION

Ghent University Conference
Brussels, 24 January 2008

PANEL DISCUSSION

Marc De Vos:
We've completed an analysis here, both in macro and micro terms, the debate in relation to the function of the market, the relationship with employment policy and labour protection and the crystallizing force of two cases which certainly have received mixed reviews.

Maybe we can start by asking the social parties for their respective reactions to these two cases. You heard some recommendations from one of our speakers on how to react and adapt to the situation. We now see a kind of additional level of interference of judges and the law with actions: something we have seen also at a national level.

So what is your assessment of that from both your perspectives?

John Monks:
I can say that there have been so many areas opened up this afternoon, that this panel won't be able to discuss them thoroughly. In response to your opening question, I will just pick the two legal cases. At the moment, we are not sure whether the effects of the two cases are a) serious or b) catastrophic in terms of a number of things. One is for the position of the unions and industrialized action in the single market – this great steamroller that powers its way into different corners of Europe and happens to have run over at least our foot in the Northern countries. We're not sure about that in relation to workers' rights. We're not sure too exactly what can be done about it and I must say that I appreciate the suggestions that have been made. I'm still not sure what can be done about it exactly either, because after the ECJ, there are not so many places to go. We are in a lot of difficulties, so much that words like "it's as bad as Bolkestein" are flying around in a lot of union debating halls, not noted for the understatement – I have to confess – but nonetheless the sense that somewhere back in the late 19th century where we were in labour law terms, but in the context of Europe. If we take the British example, some of you know originally the industrial action in Britain was regarded as a strike, as 'restrained trade' which is the old English for it. And now we are reaching the single market in two rather important cases. And although these are transnational cases (they're not perhaps the normal run of the industrial action mill) the extent to which transnationalism is affecting everything – my social partner being his usual polite self – I think the effect to what extent the transnational dimensions can be easily brought into particular disputes may well

increase as the result of these two cases. So I'm not sanguine about this line between the national and the international and the European level question. So we are extremely concerned and looking at the moment for what to do about it. I think in a way that the Swedish probably know what to do about it, and that is that they are going to change their system. They are going to deal with the positive Workers Directive, which they haven't dealt with before and so on. But the implications for the rest of us, which requires a decision that has been very well described earlier on, are the issues from which we are far from clear on exactly what to do. The issue I particularly want to tell you about is how it looks from our perspective for the moment and this is a more sober case than some of the cases that you'll hear.

Firstly, there is a specific country dimension as to how they are affected. And there is an irony in this. With regard to Marc's little speech about flexicurity there, the principles may have some American origin; they may have some Swedish origin from active labour market policy. Particularly Denmark has been the place that they've been based on. But Denmark and Sweden have identical systems and Laval could have happened in Denmark. And they are the two countries which have got to change their systems the most and they are the examples of flexicurity at the present time that the Commission and others, indeed the social partners, have been exhorting some of the lessons of the Nordic model, which I do believe is successful and which I admire greatly, have now been put at some risk. Maybe they can change themselves; maybe they can't. I don't know. They are fairly confident that they can, because there is quite a wide measure of agreement across the political parties and I think across the key social partners as well.

The second level is the European level and it's the full fundamental freedoms really: the freedom in relation to goods, services, capital and labour that we are now dealing with. The issue in Laval, which is not particularly on a Swedish level, is about the freedom of services and location of services against the union's ability to take industrial action. In an economy that is more and more international, and more and more certainly single market-based, but well beyond the single-based market, I think that more than 50% of German shareholdings are now owned outside Germany and if you go to Britain and probably Belgium as well, there is far more foreign involvement than that. You can see that it's very easy to find an international context for many of the actions, and I think that's what now we will see as a result if these two cases which have given the green light for others to be brought under European labour law more and more. There are masses of migrant workers about, by the way – someone said it earlier, just to put it slightly differently – when André Sapir and others were trying to show that there was no European social model, there was one fundamental principle of a European social model and that is free movement of labour around the European Union and some associated countries. That's the origin of the European social model and we have been living with this contradiction between national systems of industrialization and the free movement of labour until we now have a situation whereby the European Union can prize a lot of people who are very poor and can travel west very quickly since 2004. In a sense, it was there before in Spain and Portugal and maybe perhaps in Italy, but it was in a context where unemployment was not such a problem and the issue was not on the same scale. So in a lot of the disputes we're aware of, there is often a migrant dimension which is now embraced by these cases. So I anticipate more of these cases will appear. If you ask the Belgian trade union colleagues here: "would you swap the Belgian system with some designed federal European industrialization system". Then I think the answer would be no and that would be the answer from virtually every country so far. We prefer to keep it as it is; we've built it up so far since 1945. We're proud of it, we like it as it is and we do not want to change it into some unknown future. So there is not an easy option, even in the trade union world of jumping up to some federalistic labour code which is designed to get the balance right between the single market and labour standards. You then get into the argument "is it the United States of Europe or not", and all the arguments on the EU constitution and the EU reform treaty. More pragmatically, and this is my closing remark, I think having a cool headed judgment on these cases, whether it is a knock back that can be dealt with relatively easily or whether it is much worse than that, it is almost beyond our ability to correct. Whether it is, and this is my favourite subject with my social partner, hedge funds, private acuity, pirating around the world, or sovereign well funds being invited, all things that are going on in financial capitalism, plus the fact that there are 27 countries, can we reach an agreement on what to do? The political option is not an easy one and now it's probably more difficult that it has ever been. So is it serious or is it catastrophic? We'll have another one of these sessions in about three months' time and then I'll be a bit clearer on the matter than I was this afternoon.

MDV:
Apprehensive and with some fear, Business Europe chairs the new year's conference?

Philippe de Buck:
No, global capitalism is a little bit less glamorous today than it was a couple of months ago, so perhaps that's an argument vs. John Monks.

I will start where John ended. That is really the internal market because I heard different things here this afternoon on the internal market. Firstly, it is not only an economical project; it's a political one with social effects. It's the most important success factor of the European Union. It has integrated the European market, has created companies which can compete on a world level, has created

– by the way – a lot of jobs, millions of jobs that we wouldn't have had without the internal market. So the internal market is the key element. But the internal market is not only an internal market for goods, it's an internal market for capital, i.e. in the making I would say, it's an internal market for services, i.e. something that we have debated a lot. Unfortunately, we are only half way and we will see how the Member States implement the Services Directive and we have of course an internal market not for jobs, but for persons. And we claim also that all over the European Union with 27 Members States, we have opened those markets. This has of course consequences. But one of the consequences of the internal market is also to be able to face globalization and we want to make one little critical remark. If I understood you well, professor, you are being a little bit ironic about the Lisbon strategy. We are too – by the way – because it's far from finished. But the strategy is right and I want to remind you, because you have China and India, but the EU is still far from being the number one economy in the world, even with the 27 countries together. Secondly comes of course the United States and far behind is China. So the strategy to be the number one in the world, the most competitive in society is to have more and better jobs, because this you haven't mentioned, is the right strategy and we hope that this strategy will continue, even after 2010. It's far from over – a lot has to be done.

On flexicurity, I would like to say....... unless you want me to come back to that later?

MDV:
Could you give your comment on the cases?

Philippe de Buck:
On the cases, I'm not able, even if I was a lawyer, to dispute all the legal arguments. I think the case was unfair. The best argument was given just a few minutes ago by John Monks. Since the national system has to be changed because of the European system, the case was unfair. If we don't accept, in an internal market, that companies can work elsewhere, then we had better stop. And that was what was on the basis. Of course you have, based on the posting of the Workers Directive, to respect the rules of the countries where you operate. That is also something that we as Business Europe have defended and therefore that the Services Directive of Bolkestein was right, because it was linked to the Posting of the Workers Directive and avoided social dumping, but of course you have to know the rules. And more than that, the rules have to exist. If there is not a minimum wage, how can you deal with the minimum wage? If the agreements have not been made universally applicable, then how can you deal with that? So a company has to deal with the rules it is confronted with and that was, in our view at least, the case. Therefore we can dispute who will have to look on proportionality,

but the action/strike against a foreign company who wants to participate in a public tender or contract is not right. Will it have consequences? I think so: it will have consequences more at a national level than at a European level, but I don't fear it at all. It's serious but not catastrophic. It's serious because we have to make the companies and people able to work in the other Member States. If that is not made possible, we have a problem.

MDV:
Thank you. I'd like to pass to the politician here.

EU Employment has been a player in this debate and is, as Mr. Monks pointed out, fueled by enlargement, migration, etc. The European parliament has played an important role in the discussion of the Services Directive, so can you give us some views and of course your own voice on the way the European parliament is confronting these issues which are all about the combination of labour and the internal market?

Dirk Sterckx:
There is one thing that struck me about what Mr. Monks said and that is that at some point the Court of Justice will move in. And what do we do then? When does the Court of Justice move in? It moves in when we as politicians haven't done our job – when there is no clear law for a judge to decide what is legal and what is not. Then there are other cases where the Court of Justice, and not just in social affairs, shakes the tree. I think it was in 1985 when Parliament went to court to ask to prosecute the Council for not taking any action with regard to transport policy. The court decided that the Council had to move and it moved. The same thing happened to health care where the Member States and their very powerful organisations and of course important budgetary balances had to be kept. There the Court of Justice said in a number of cases that there are other things to consider. It is not just your national interest and the balance of your social system that counts. There are other things. The same example is the equal treatment of men and women. So when the rules are not clear and when politicians are not able to make clear rules, the Court of Justice moves in. If we can avoid it, we should avoid it. The thing here and also with the Services Directive.........

MDV:
So you are pleading for a direction on collective action or something like that?

Dirk Sterckx:
That is one of the discussions and I'm glad that Parliament has been able to make a compromise on the Services Directive because when I was in Belgium involved in the discussion as a member of the European Parliament, I must say that I didn't

get much help at the Belgian level – neither from the union nor from business organisations. There was not very much constructive advice on how to solve the problem. The only advice we got was voted down, made to disappear, as if the problem would disappear, which of course didn't happen, because the problem exists in the real world, whether it be legal or illegal. You can talk about migrants, but some of them are illegal. And they won't go away because we say they shouldn't be there. So I'm glad that with the Services Directive, Parliament was able to make a compromise (that was not to everybody's liking), but that's the way a compromise is reached. So it's there and it's a first step.

So my second question is, everybody shoots at the single market and says, "look what this is doing to us". It's not only a source of economic growth and jobs. The general question is: do we want to be open or not as an economy? And there, globalisation plays a part: the protection vs. openness. What is going to profit us most? And that is a question that is always there, whether it be in our internal cross-border relationships or whether it be in our cross-border relationship with countries like Brazil or China. And one of the things I would like to learn as a politician from the learned peoples of the universities, is, what are the consequences of openness historically? What is the consequence of the single market? We've had it for 15 years now more or less, since 1992. Was it so bad? Where are the disasters? I remember the discussion when I was a journalist before 1992, when some people said that if you open up this whole thing, there is going to be a disaster. It was less threatening and much more specific for goods than for services. But I haven't heard many points of argument against the Services Directive. Most of them were emotional and not based on analyses of sectors with figures in it, saying, look, we are talking about these kinds of movements. One thing I've once asked an economist is to tell me what were the consequences of the several phases in which the Belgian economy opened up: first the Benelux, then in 1957 the treaty of Rome, then the different steps in which the EU market evolved, with enlargement into the single market in 1992 and so on. There are not many figures on that. I didn't get a clear overview of what the consequences were. The general idea is that every phase of opening up shook up the system and was painful. We had a phase of adaptation and change and getting things back to normal. But after that phase, there was economic growth and there was growth in social spending as well. In each of these phases, I think this is what we are going to see with opening up of services. One of the sectors that was opposed to it, was the building sector in Belgium. They were the ones who were apprehensive towards the FBO/FVB, together with the interim sector. For opposite reasons, yes, but they were the ones who convinced the whole organisation to be against it. It took the organisation a year to change its mind and to come back to the real figures. Then I spoke to people who were responsible for building projects in big international companies and that were doing buildings in all countries in the EU and also outside the EU:

the United States, Australia and so on. The man, a Flemish person who was responsible in this huge company for building projects, said that the most efficient and productive companies in industrial building, are Belgian. They do the fastest and cheapest projects. Not the Poles, not the British – the British were one of the worst – and I always wondered, and afterwards I went back to ask for figures, why are we so afraid of opening up this part of the services market, if we are the strongest ones in the market? So it is very difficult for us as politicians once the emotional debate has started, to go back to the figures. And there are so few figures available on the real situation of what the consequences could be of opening up. This is something I missed very much in the debate on the Services Directive. So it's an ideological choice to choose between openness and protection. And I see that most of the time the first reaction is protection. The Commission made its proposals yesterday on how to deal with energy, efficiency and CO_2. One of the reactions now is that maybe we should bring in the Globalisation Fund if the consequences are that we are losing jobs. So the first thing is, how can we protect ourselves against a move forward and that's one thing as a politician of course, that you have to face these emotional reactions but there is not enough hard evidence of what social reality in fact is and what social progress is, not only in the short term, because there are movements, but in the long term, and how we can convince people to accept change and to work towards quicker change. Because I'm convinced that societies that adapt in the best way to change are the ones that are going to survive best and you can do it the cruel way, the way the United States do it. If you do it the cruel way, if you don't have any real social security, you fall out. We have another kind of system and the Scandinavians have the most developed one. I think it's better to have our system and openness hasn't harmed it, so I'm looking forward to hearing more from the academic world to support my view.

MDV:
Thank you for the suggestion. We will take it with us as we prepare the book. I would like to bring in the Commission here. The Commission of course is an actor in both of the cases and is also a broker for this evolution of change, single market review which was highlighted at the beginning – the flexicurity development. So your views on both of the cases are welcome, and then bringing it forward to the evolution of a single market and employment policy, I would like then to have the social partners intervene.

Armindo Silva:
If you allow me, I would prefer to divert the issues and to make a point about the Services Directive. Of course the two rulings are very important and the Commission is examining them very closely in order to draw operational

conclusions which we have not yet done, so my opinions are here purely personal.

I wonder whether those rulings can be considered as marking a kind of paradigm in the case law. Are they going to have a fundamental impact on the EU social model and the way the EU rules interact with the national rules? Are we witnessing a tectonic shift? I'm convinced of this. And I want to go back to the hype that was expressed before, surrounding these two cases to the timing and simultaneity with the discussion on the Services Directive and the referenda. 2005 was the year when the discussion was hotter in Parliament and when the case was referred to the EU Court of Justice. And of course there was an interaction certainly on certain provisions that were introduced in Parliament concerning labour law that reflected some fears that have been generated in the framework of the Laval case. And the way the whole anxiety exists still has in mind the very much ideological discussions that surrounded the Services Directive. There was in particular one underlying line of consensus that emerged in the end, and that was the need to keep labour law out. Everybody of course knows that the Services Directive, even after the version that was approved in the end, is going to have considerable effects on the market. The proportion between the share of tradable services, which is about 40%, and the share of real trade within the union on services offers a very large scope for impact in terms of prices, costs, and of course labour standards and labour conditions. There was a consensus that this impact, which some would say in these terms was positive for jobs, was a market economic study that estimated the overall impact of the Services Directive before, at about 37 billion euros of net gain for welfare and 600,000 jobs. Most of it will be kept unchallenged by the changes that were introduced in the freedom to provide a services chapter that will be responsible for about one third of the quantity of this impact. So the impact is going to be very large, both in macro-economic terms and micro-economic terms and on labour standards, independently of whether or not labour law is left aside. Prof. Barnard already mentioned Article 1 of the Services Directive. Also Article 16 §3 reinvents to some extent labour law. The problem is that in most service markets competition happens between undertakings employing employees and self-employed people who are not bound by collective agreements ordered by law. And this is different from what happens in goods markets where competition is mostly undertaken between companies. So of course this will certainly create a situation for particularly those sectors which are heavily protected, for companies and for self-employed people to the extent that a number of administrative and legal barriers will disappear with the implementation of directives. There will be greater competition and there will be a possibility of those sectors where hand seeking is perhaps excessive. There will be a tendency towards a cut of wages and working conditions independently of what we define in terms of labour law because many of the competitors are not bound by it. Of course this creates a problem for labour law, both in national and EU labour law. In the first place to the extent that this may contribute to further erosion of the employment relationship, companies will be led more and more to avoid employment contracts, to avoid employment relationships and to develop ingenious forms of creating self-employed situations. There is of course a grey area which is increasing and might increase more and more with the services directive as a result of it. This is not only a problem for national labour law but also for EU labour law to the extent that our directives apply to employees, to people who have an employment relationship in Member States. Therefore this erosion affects also the scope of application of community law and may create an artificial disadvantage in terms of competition. Imagine a country that applies very loose criteria for the definition of the self-employed and others, and others that are more strict. We might have a problem here. That's why we identify the issue of employment relationship as one of the key issues of our paper on labour law and we identify it also as one of the priorities to do further work in the years ahead and we intend to conduct further analysis and monitoring of the situation in Member States. I think this has to do of course with the impact of the Services Directive.

On the Laval case I would first say that it's a balanced judgment to the extent that it recognises the right to take collective action as a fundamental right and confirms that the trade unions continue to be able to take action to protect workers' interests and combat social lacking. Of course provided that this is not in compliance with the treaty and the general principles of community law, but in the national legal order also, collective action is restrained by law and by constitution in all cases as far as I know. So we feel that the overall ruling is balanced and it is also a very welcome judgment to the extent that it brings important clarifications to two open issues of interpretation of the directive on posting of workers. Firstly, it clearly states that the purpose of Directive 96 71 on posting of workers is not to harmonise systems for establishing terms and conditions of employment. Therefore the Member States keep their freedom to choose a system which is not expressly mentioned in the directive, provided that it does not hinder the free provision of services. Therefore, Sweden cannot be considered to infringe the directive, because it has not notified its intention to apply the option provided in §8 of Article 3, which relates to the possibility of collective agreements that are generally applicable, all concluded by the representative partners. The second point of clarification, is that the level of protection that must be guaranteed to posted workers, is limited to the core of mandatory holds for minimum protection of workers that is defined in §1C of Article 3 of the directive, unless those workers are enjoying a more favourable protection in the country of origin. This is an important clarification which is justified by the argument that the directive would have been deprived of its effectiveness if the host Member State could go beyond this core of mandatory holds and apply fully its national employment law. I think that we should record that the directive is intended to offer protection to workers who are temporarily posted in a country and not to be included permanently as part of the labour market. I think that this makes a very important distinction to understand the philosophy of this directive. The clarification of the Court was essentially in this respect.

Of course more controversial is the court's allegation to choose the setting of minimum wage that is not transparent, that provokes uncertainty and the result of the method shows that the wages effectively applied to workers are not minimum wages and are above the minimum level of wages. Therefore they do not comply with Article 3 §1. Of course the court here develops arguments that the Commission has to take into account because it represents a development on the basis in relation to what the Commission has stated.

Finally the Court has found that the Swedish law, so-called Lex Britannia, does not pass the criterion of non-discrimination, because it allows the unions to take action against foreign service providers in order to sign collective agreements, even if the service provider already has a collective agreement in the country of origin, whereas collective action is not allowed against a Swedish company in the same situation. There is a clear case of discrimination here. The ball now is in the court of the Swedish government, which has to assess the effects of this link on its legislation. I wonder if some Member States will also carefully study the results to the extent that they have similar systems of collective agreements in industrial relations, Denmark being one of them, has authorities who would be also interested to study closely the ruling. Of course we will continue to cooperate with those authorities in order to help them to have a reaction that is proportional to the importance of the ruling.

MDV:
Thank you, so the Commission at least welcomes the clarifications and moves on.

I would like to conclude with the social partners. A number of fundamental issues have been raised here by the development, single market, social policy, employment, flexicurity and crystallising around these cases, so very briefly: how do you see the future? What's the future for social policy from your perspective in the EU?

Philippe de Buck:
Well, trying to summarise, firstly, we favour the European model. We favour the European model because you have 27 social systems. The European social model: what does it mean? When you have economic growth, part of it goes to more

solidarity. And you have it even in the U.K. and everywhere. In different ways, but that is the basis. It is based also on social dialogue. So we favour also social dialogue. We do that on a European level, but of course most of the social dialogue is on company level, because it starts with a contract between a company and a worker. And on branch level I will not go into detail. Therefore, flexicurity is key. And why is flexicurity key? By the way, as another argument that has not been touched here, it is because you not only have to manage the change, you also have to manage the ageing populations and the cost related to that.

www.ingramcontent.com/pod-product-compliance
Ingram Content Group UK Ltd.
Pitfield, Milton Keynes, MK11 3LW, UK
UKHW051928100926
8556IPUK00022B/1427

9 789050 959148